The BELLEVUE BOTANICAL GARDEN

Celebrating the First 15 Years

DEAR MR. KARLE,
THANK YOU FOR YOUR
SUPPORT OF THE GARDEN.

Bob Cromwell
BBGS PRESIDENT

I loved telling this story!
Marty Wingate

The BELLEVUE BOTANICAL GARDEN

Celebrating the First 15 Years

Published by
The Bellevue Botanical Garden Society

MISSION STATEMENT

The **Bellevue Botanical Garden** develops, maintains, and displays plant collections in a park setting for the purposes of research, horticultural demonstration, and passive recreation. It provides a forum for public education in botany, horticulture, and related fields.

Community involvement at many levels of **Garden** operations is a fundamental goal and is essential to the **Garden's** continuing development and maintenance.

Table of Contents

Great things are not done by impulse, but by a series of small things brought together. Vincent van Gogh

A SERIES OF SMALL THINGS

It may seem to some a significant disjuncture that I find the inspiration to write while in the mountains of far northern Vietnam, specifically in the hill town of Sa Pa. In contrast to the oppressive steaminess of Hanoi, here there is a delicious breeze and gossamer quality to the air, as I look across a valley of neatly terraced paddies and an enormous mountain rising in the distance.

I am able to pause in this unlikely place to contemplate the forthcoming celebration of the first 15 years of the Bellevue Botanical Garden. In the short span of one and a half decades, this endeavor has not only flourished in a physical sense, but also has been anointed the showcase of Pacific Northwest horticulture. In our modified Mediterranean climate, which allows such an enormous inventory of plants to be successfully cultivated, BBG has at last put a polish to the jewel of the greater Puget Sound region.

So I sit to ponder this success, so many thousands of miles away, as the weather I experience here precisely mimics that which had settled over the Northwest upon my departure this autumn. Even with the excitement ahead, of seeing the staggeringly rich botanical inventory of this portion of the planet, it is never easy to leave home. This is especially true at that time of year when the temperatures and slant of sun and caliber of light reach an apogee of perfection.

For a moment again, this morning in Sa Pa, I can briefly re-experience that which I am missing, sans, of course, the endearing bits of home and garden. The whole of our region, marine and mountain, rain forest and high desert, with a rich and colorful overlay of indigenous culture, seems too intricate to describe in a condensed, abbreviated fashion. My recognition of and obligation to the benign parameters under which I garden are nearly heartrending. And so, it seems, it makes it somewhat easier to be removed from it entirely to adequately write of it.

As a youthful gardener, I was subjected to the Calvinistic Zone 4 highlands of north-central Michigan. It was a particularly cruel landscape for an adventurous gardener. I remember persuading my parents to buy a not-inexpensive (20 bucks, 1967) specimen of *Magnolia* × *soulangeana* for their garden. I watched it freeze-dry in our subzero temperatures that first winter with considerable embarrassment, while listening to the silence of my parents' displeasure.

After 27 years of severe climatic discipline, I landed in Western Washington. In that first winter, I encountered fragrance and flowers at a most unnatural time of year. Those who have never been deprived of flowers in the landscape in the winter might possess no appreciation of the value of that gift. For that gratitude alone, I am glad to have been deprived, as those indulged with such things in their youth might always take such pleasures for granted.

Yet a seemingly perfect climate for gardening does not make a garden. There, too, must exist a community of the like-minded in which to share — plants and what can be achieved by combining them just so, how to mulch and maintain, prune and propagate. In this matter, the Pacific Northwest, too, has excelled. Whether our benevolent climate is responsible for this camaraderie, or if the planets simply aligned appropriately for a short order, it does not really matter. There exists an aggregate of numerous organizations and societies that invites and then lifts the nascent passions of a beginning gardener.

When I was younger and beginning to garden seriously, I misinterpreted this eager quality of our local horticultural collective as unabashed competition. As I have matured, I have come to realize that although accomplishment can often come by way of mild intimidation, good gardens cannot be achieved by one-upmanship. Perhaps I came round to that way of thinking after encountering a French aphorism that, although was meant to apply to the creation of music, has comparable relevance to making gardens. "On ne fait pas de musique contre quelqu'un" ("One does not make music against someone else"). The societies devoted to plants and their study in our region provide an accessible and inviting opportunity for all of those wishing to learn.

With climate and community in such ample volume, and in sync with a legion of legendary nurseries and garden centers, the Pacific Northwest morphed during the past two decades into not only the Western hub of North American horticulture, but also in numerous ways its nucleus. Yet within this frenzied state of green, there existed a gaping hole with the general absence or incongruity of public horticulture. In a region with not only such ludicrous potential, but also with also a deliberate Olmstedian intent, the greater Puget Sound area still appeared, at least in terms of public spaces, very early Gold Rush.

This was especially true if one looked to the north, in Vancouver, B.C., with three established, well-executed, and highly regarded plant collections for the edification of the public: VanDusen Botanical Garden, University of British Columbia Botanical Garden, and Queen Elizabeth Park. In Seattle, on the other hand, Washington Park Arboretum, our only significant public garden of note, had lost its focus, and funding became inadequate. Though there has never been a shortage of the civic-minded in the Northwest, the visual and performing arts seemed to gather the lion's share of private funding.

During my first winter in Seattle, then, nearly 25 years ago, it was intriguing to hear the stirrings of a new botanical garden in Bellevue. There dwells in all of us, I believe, the skeptic, and despite the charge conjured by the simple notion that someone thought it possible, my own inner skeptic was awakened. Could anyone remotely understand the degree of dedication and resources required to successfully carry out such a pipe dream? Especially so if spearheaded by the general citizenry without the anointment of university affiliation.

In retrospect, I now wonder why I thought that great gardens and preserved spaces happened by any other means. As it is, there is no perfect beginning for any ultimate success, only a dogged persistence. Those who chose to press on from that first improbable gathering in Bellevue, creating in the process a unique model in affiliating so closely with local horticultural societies, were acutely aware of the lasting power of public spaces as well as the seductive ease of asphalt, concrete, and quick profit.

So here I am, the quieted and humbled observer of a now first-class institution. I am still gazing out upon a mountainside near Sa Pa, with rice crops taking on the gild of autumn, dogs incessantly barking, and the high-voltage buzz of cicadas in the distance. And deliberating, as I write this, not only how very grateful I am to have stumbled into the horticultural milieu of the Pacific Northwest, but also for the visionaries and generous spirits that believed such a garden should and would happen. On the 15th anniversary of its inception, this garden is now the catalyst in polishing the jewel that is our region to the luminosity it has long deserved.

Daniel J. Hinkley
Sa Pa, North Vietnam
October 14, 2006

The
Vision

The Vision

"The Shorts created great impetus for us. ... It was the right thing at the right time. ..."

The roots of today's Garden lie in its past and in its people. Before there was a Bellevue Botanical Garden, there was farmland, a cherry orchard, and — further back — a logging settlement. The Garden is built on history and exists today because of the people who cared and worked to fashion a living jewel. The Garden was created out of the love for plants, gardens, and open spaces. Today's Garden is the result of hard work, generous volunteers, foresight, and not a little bit of serendipity. Here is its story.

WILBURTON HILL

At the beginning, the land seemed endless. Bellevue was a small
town until well into the 1950s. Across the water, Seattle was growing
by leaps and bounds, filling all available space. Bellevue's population
in 1950 was 8,000, already a leap because the first floating bridge had
opened in 1940. In the 1940s and 1950s, large tracts of land still existed, and open spaces still existed there into the 1970s, including an area
just east of the old downtown known as Wilburton Hill.

Wilburton Hill began life as a settlement with a mill. The neighborhood had been known as Wilbur's town, or Wilburton. At the turn
of the 20th century, Manley Wilbur ran a lumber mill on the Mercer
Slough, which at that time was deeper than today; logs could be towed
from the mill's dock out into Lake Washington and then to Seattle. But
in 1916, the Montlake cut was dug to connect Lake Washington to Lake
Union and then to open water. The water level in the lake dropped dra-
matically, and the mill, left high and dry, could no longer send its logs
off to Seattle.

Despite the setback to the Wilburton mill, the area continued to
grow, although separately from its big-city neighbor across the lake. But

when the first floating bridge opened in 1940 — and then when the toll was lifted in 1946 — Bellevue became an easy commute from Seattle. That encouraged people to move out of the city in which they worked. The original estimates that 2,000 cars a day would use the bridge were far below the reality; as soon as it opened, 5,000 cars made the daily trip. The population in Bellevue took an upswing. The 1950 Census showed 8,000 residents. That jumped to 12,800 in 1960 and 73,902 by 1980.

The neighborhood of Wilburton Hill had some commanding views of the area during the decades before the second growth of Douglas firs, Western red cedars, and Western hemlocks began to fill in. The forest was kept at bay on the hill around scattered farmhouses and cabins.

CAL AND HARRIET SHORTS

It was just such a cabin that caught Cal Shorts' eye in 1946. The land was still mostly rural, which suited Calhoun and Harriet Shorts just fine; in fact, it was what they were seeking — a piece of land in the country upon which they could grow food

LEFT **Life on Wilburton Hill** FROM TOP **Hewitt and Lea sawmill, circa 1903; logging train; Wilburton trestle, on the site of the Hewitt and Lea sawmill.** RIGHT **Harriet and son Binkley sit in front of their cabin.**

and ornamental plants. The couple lived in Bellevue, and Cal worked at The Boeing Co. in Renton — one of many careers that included lawyer, teacher, and inventor. Keeping their eyes out for a likely plot, Cal came across a cabin and cherry orchard while he was driving to and from work. It wasn't long before they owned 7 acres, cabin, chickens, pigpen, and assorted farm paraphernalia. It was there they tried their hand at country living.

During the almost 30 years they lived there, Cal and Harriet Shorts with son Binkley first raised cows, goats, and other animals, but gradually they became more interested in plants. Cal was an active member of the Puget Sound Beekeepers Association; that is just one example of what a great interest both Cal and Harriet had in plants and nature. They took a turn at hybridizing and growing rhododendrons, became members of the Cascade chapter of the American Rhododendron Society, and in the late 1950s worked with Halfdan Lem, who was well-known throughout the rhododendron community for his work crossing rhododendrons. An

unregistered peach-colored cultivar that Cal called 'Harriet' can still be found in the Garden.

The log cabin gave way to a house that Cal and Harriet had built in 1957. The house was in the modern Northwest style with Asian influence, designed by architect Paul Kirk, and it stands today, as the Shorts Visitor Center. It was quite a step up from the insect-infested log cabin.

By the early 1980s, the Wilburton neighborhood had been mostly settled, but 100 acres remained on the hill. Among the local residents who used the area, walking the social trails that ran throughout the space, were Iris and Bob Jewett. They and their neighbors began to hear talk that development would go in — maybe a retirement center, possibly office buildings. Lee Springgate, director of the Parks and Recreation Department in Bellevue at the time, says the 40 acres the City had assembled around the property the Shortses owned were to be used for a government center. Residents of the Wilburton neighborhood rallied, organized, and united to let the City know that they wanted green

ABOVE **The log cabin deteriorated during Cal and Harriet's 10 years there, and so they had a new house built on almost the same site in 1957.** TOP **The house Cal and Harriet had built to replace the cabin was designed by** Paul Kirk, **a well-known architect who specialized in a Northwest version of the modern style, known for its sleek, streamlined forms and post-and-beam design.**

space kept green. They saw the value of the land left as open space and knew that it was not possible to get back the land once it had been developed.

Residents appeared at City Council meetings and struck a visual chord by dressing all in black and white to appear as a cohesive group; they even carried balloons. The neighbors' united voice was heard, as they began appearing at council meetings to urge the council members to hold onto the green space they had.

THE IDEA OF A GARDEN

Then the stars, it seemed, aligned. Plans to develop the 40 acres the City owned were dropped, in part because Cal and Harriet — and by this time Cal was a member of the Park Board — did not want to sell their land just to see it be developed. Instead, they offered it to the City as part of a park, if the City would add an adjacent 10 acres. Cal and Harriet's holdout was part of what sparked the idea of park space and came in part from Harriet's memory of her father's work helping to develop the parks in Spokane. Cal Shorts was what Lee Springgate calls "a renaissance man," and not just because of all of his various professions. "He wanted his property to go for some valuable social purpose — he and Harriet both did."

So, a park was on the agenda, but until the Jewetts spoke up, no one mentioned a botanical garden. "I remember as clear as if it was yesterday them coming into my office in Kelsey Creek with what I thought was this half-baked idea of a botanical garden," Lee says. But the Jewetts persisted, and Bob stood up at a council meeting and asked the same question — "Why not a garden?" They knew what a botanical garden could mean to the City.

Iris and Bob had long enjoyed the look and feel of VanDusen Botanical Garden in Vancouver, British Columbia. That garden was made on land that had been a golf course and contained open strolling spaces and planted ornamental gardens throughout its 55 acres. It was an example of a large garden in the middle of a city — and the City of Bellevue was coming up to Wilburton Hill's doorstep. Could a garden be created there?

While campaigning to save Wilburton Hill as a park, and perhaps a garden, the Jewetts heard that Cal and Harriet had donated 7.5 acres of their own land to the City to be kept as a park. Another example of happenstance, perhaps, but everyone agrees that these events were all influenced by the atmosphere of the day, when civic-

Iris and Bob Jewett

The Jewetts are called the founders of the Bellevue Botanical Garden, and for good reason: As residents of the Wilburton Hill neighborhood, they were persistent in their idea for a botanical garden in the park, and they approached Cal and Harriet Shorts with the idea. Everyone agrees that Cal and Harriet were ecstatic with the idea and the outcome. The Jewetts moved to Bellevue in 1979. At that time, Iris remembers, there were still sheep kept on Wilburton Hill, and horses in the neighborhood were common. They brought with them the idea that parks are important in cities, and their vision paid off.

To honor their commitment and work, in 1996 Iris and Bob were named Citizens of the Year by the International Northwest Parks and Recreation Association. They are known as the founders of the Garden, as well they should be. The Jewetts still live in the Wilburton neighborhood, creating weather-resistant artistic pots and artwork for the garden through their business, Wilburton Pottery.

> "Public gardens that create a focus for a neighborhood or a town can become community gathering places in which people take pride. They also serve as training grounds for gardeners, garden maintenance people, arborists, and other would-be gardeners." Nancy Davidson Short

minded citizens wanted to build and shape a town into a livable city. The Jewetts decided to go and talk with Cal and Harriet Shorts about their land.

"We sat in their back yard at a picnic table," says Iris, "on a beautiful sunny day, and we said to them, 'What do you think about creating a botanical garden on your land?'"

From such a small act, big things were born. Cal and Harriet Shorts were immediately on board for the Garden. "Lee said, 'Sure you can have a botanical garden, if you find other people to help,'" Iris remembers. The Jewetts knew they must gather up a committed group, and so they plastered the area with notices of a meeting at the Bellevue library. Iris remembers that 25 people showed up for that first gathering in October 1984, and the Garden was on its way.

The City of Bellevue was committed to creating a livable city by keeping open spaces and establishing parks. Mayor Cary Bozeman and park Director Lee Springgate were happy to have an enthusiastic group that was willing to take charge of creating a garden in the park. The creation of a botanical garden within the larger Wilburton Hill Park became one of the options on the master plan for the space, and everyone liked it. Wilburton Hill Park became part of what the City saw as a neo-Olmstedian park system — green spaces, boulevards, and parks connected and connecting Lake Washington to Lake Sammamish.

THE GARDEN BECOMES A REALITY

A partnership was formed between the City and the Society and between the City and horticultural groups that develop

and maintain some of the display gardens within the botanical garden. The result is a showcase that is supported in time and money from volunteers and city workers who are committed to education and display. "Cal and Harriet were the catalyst;

the Jewetts were the founders," Springgate says. "With political support from the City and the public support," the Garden took shape. A task force began to set priorities, and plans began.

The land acquisition came first. To the

LEFT **The land that Cal and Harriet bought had an old cherry orchard, with some trees up to 50 years old.**

"It's a partnership you won't find anywhere else in the country." Jerry Nissley

The Bellevue Botanical Garden, which is part of Wilburton Hill Park, is owned by the City and is run as one of its parks. City staffers work as manager and gardeners, while a volunteer organization, the Bellevue Botanical Garden Society, works as a support organization. That includes fundraising and helping to make decisions about the displays and the Garden.

A coordinating committee, made up of several members of the Society and several people from the City of Bellevue, acts as a liaison, ensuring that communication flows smoothly between the two. The Society is able to keep abreast of decisions made by the City about the Garden, and the City knows about events the Society runs.

In addition to the partnership between the City and the Society, the City formed partnerships with horticultural organizations on the development and maintenance of some of the individual Garden displays within the whole Garden. Interested organizations contact the parks department. City representatives take the proposal to the coordinating committee, where the entire plan is reviewed. After terms of the partnership are agreed upon, the organization and the City sign a contract. The Northwest Perennial Alliance Borders and the Fuchsia Garden are examples of that kind of partnership.

7.5 acres donated by Cal and Harriet for a garden, the City added more land, and eventually 28.5 acres, so that the Garden and park together amounted to 36 acres set within the larger Wilburton Hill Park, which consists of a total of 105 acres. Much later 17 acres were added.

How do you get from an idea of a garden to its reality? And a public garden, at that. Our home gardens are of our own devising — or that of a designer we hire. We configure our private space to suit ourselves, without any regard for the possibility that thousands may want to walk through. But a public garden must take into account heavy foot traffic, where that foot traffic will go, and what visitors will view.

The design of a public garden takes into account not just plants and paths, but also how and why to get from one place to another. How to draw people in without jeopardizing the very plants they have come to see. How to meet the expectations of those who know much about gardens while still pleasing, occupying, and engaging those who know little or nothing about plants.

A master plan gives a comprehensive

ABOVE **Harriet later recalled many of the old varieties of cherries that were on the land, including 'Bing', 'Lambert', 'Black Tartarian', and 'Royal Ann'.**

RIGHT **The entrance plaza was designed by the Bellevue firm JGM. Although elements would change over the years, the true focus of the Garden remained to create a world-class botanical garden.**

developmental guide, and it may include detailed or conceptual drawings. Jongejan Gerrard McNeal (now JGM), a landscape architecture firm in Bellevue, created the original master plan for Wilburton Hill Park, which included a botanical garden. From the original intention, a public garden was made.

What does the Garden look like, and why? How do you make a public garden? Iain Robertson, landscape architect and University of Washington professor, has studied the struggle of public gardens. It is the pull between accessibility and beautiful scenes. And along with that goes the theme of a botanical garden as a place to demonstrate plants and design to home gardeners, plus the happy problem of how to incorporate the benefits of the existing landscape. The legacy of Cal and Harriet is not only in the land itself, but also in the plant life.

The original design was completed in the summer of 1989 by Robertson and Bellevue project manager John Barker. Iain Robertson had designed the landscape a few years before at the UW's Center for Urban Horticulture. One leg of what is now called the Lake to Lake Trail in Bellevue looked as if it might pass through the middle of the Garden, but the designers urged the City to route the path around instead of through, so that the Garden would remain whole instead of divided into halves.

Not only did that keep the Garden whole, but it also allowed for the design of the first main way to walk through the Garden: the loop trail. The first drawings show the emphasis on circulation in the form of the loop trail, which would draw visitors from the visitor center, along the large border display created and maintained by the Northwest Perennial Alliance, down around the wetland ponds, up alongside the Yao Japanese Garden, through the ground-cover garden and back to the visitor center.

Lee Springgate was director of the Parks and Recreation Department (later changed to Parks and Community Services) in Bellevue for more than 20 years. It was Lee's vision for parks and open spaces in the City that helped bring the Bellevue Botanical Garden and Wilburton Park into existence. Iain Robertson said of Lee: "He had a lot to do with broadening people's conception of what a public park could be."

Lee sees it as giving volunteers a chance. "The lesson is that if your volunteers are that competent and they work that hard, then give them plenty of leeway and encouragement, and don't try to control the product."

Those who worked with Lee Springgate during the process of creating the Garden acknowledge that it was his leadership that helped the dream come true. And no one is surprised that he continues to work with other communities on park development.

Of course, those gardens didn't exist in 1989. Some weren't even envisioned. And the construction of the trail meant 50 large, mature rhododendrons had to be moved out of the way and then moved back again. But the plan held the most important elements of a public garden and the hope the Garden would grow into a world-class destination. From that first meeting of interested people in 1984 to the first plans in 1989 and to the opening of the Garden three years later — and beyond — ideas would emerge, workers would volunteer, gardens would be created.

Would we recognize the Garden as it was on opening day, June 27, 1992? Certainly the bones were there — the loop trail and the house where the Shorts family lived for almost 30 years. The house sits well in its surroundings and with minor remodeling became a pleasant, open, sunny visitor center that includes a gift shop. The interior Shoji screens and the atrium bring the outdoors in, a perfect quality in a public building associated with a garden. The entrance patio, rill, and pond, which are a favorite of visitors, had been installed and would lead visitors to the door of the visitor center.

The entry plaza and rill were designed by the firm of JGM; Iain Robertson supervised installation. This broad, inviting area sets the scene for the Garden. For most people, the approach to the visitor center is up the steps and past a hillside of changing plant selection and design. At the top of the steps, a broad granite plaza lies between the visitor and the building, and a water feature that captures the fancy of young and old alike bisects this broad paved area. It is a rill, a tiny stream but in a formal setting. The water runs between bricks and under the feet in a narrow channel down to a pool and then circulates back again. This ingenious design is at once a visual element that draws the eye — and so the feet — toward the building and an enchanting water feature. "Look!" children and adults seem to say, "I can walk on water!"

Other buildings that either were already on the land, or were moved there, or were purpose-built became part of the Garden's landscape. Each has a job. A residence on Main Street became the caretaker's cottage and garden office. Today, the Tateuchi Pavilion is located on the spot Cal had built a garden shed with Japanese-style doors in the early 1960s; the design was copied from the teahouse in the Japanese Garden at the Washington Park Arboretum. The Sharp cabin (also known as Cottonwood cabin) was moved to the Garden in 1989. The cabin is the 1920s second-story addition to a cabin built in 1888. When the ground floor deteriorated, the Bellevue Historical Society and Scott Parker, the last renter, helped save the second story from destruction. Today, the cabin is used as a meeting space.

The years between the formation of the Society in 1984 and the opening of the Garden in 1992 were full of activity for the ever-increasing number of volunteers and Society members. The Garden was raising awareness in people's minds, and potential members were drawn from a variety of sources, including an information booth at the new Northwest Flower & Garden Show. That exposure led many new members to help with the work of creating the Garden.

Part of the alliance included the city-funded position of curator. Until one was found, the City provided an interim curator, Jerry Nissley, project manager in the resource management division for Bellevue.

ABOVE **The Sharp cabin was moved to the Garden from a site one mile north in 1989, having been saved from destruction by the Bellevue Historical Society and the cabin's last renter.**

TOP **Construction on the Garden was carried out in all weather in preparation for the June 1992 opening.**

Nancy Fonk

Working hard at a job is one thing, but when you give up the job so you can spend precious years with your children, yet remain one of the most reliable, inspirational, and dedicated volunteers, you take your commitment to a new level. When Nancy Fonk left her job as curator of the BBG, she in no way left the Garden. "I stayed active because my heartstrings wouldn't let me do otherwise!"

Nancy was inventive and resourceful, both in her paid job as curator and afterward as a volunteer. Lee Springgate approached Nancy in 1994 and said: "While I don't understand the Garden's huge success, you're doing a great job. Figure out how to get people up here in the winter." And so she thought of an outdoor light display, not with a holiday theme, but a garden theme. Garden d'Lights sprouted, and it has grown over the years just as a living garden grows.

In addition to Garden d'Lights and service on the executive committee, through the years Nancy worked on education, events, programs, and operations; she has supported garden development and fundraising planning, too. She couldn't let go of the Garden, and the Garden is better for it.

The search for a garden curator resulted in applications from such faraway places as Great Britain and Hawaii. In the summer of 1992, Nancy Fonk, the first — and, as it turned out, the only — curator of the Garden, came from working eight years at the National Tropical Botanical Gardens in Kauai and Maui, Hawaii. Nancy was the organizational head of the Bellevue Botanical Garden and the link between the Society and the City.

Nancy also realized that the job title of curator was not quite accurate. A curator manages plant collections, and Nancy was managing so much more than the plants. She was coordinating the entire volunteer force, the paid staff, and the grounds. Her three-year tenure would result in an important change in the title of the job from curator to garden manager.

As time drew near for a proposed 1992 opening, reality began to set in. The first landscaping to be completed included the loop trail — after all, visitors needed a way to see the Garden — the entrance paving and rill, the Yao Japanese Garden, and the Ground Cover Garden. The Northwest Perennial Alliance Border and Fuchsia Garden were ready, too. Different styles, different themes, different reasons for being, but all the display gardens teach, which is one part of the Society's mission statement and a key factor in botanical gardens.

The rush of excitement about the opening of the Garden could be seen on the horizon from a year away. A preview open house was held in September 1991, while most gardens were still being planned. But grand plans of gardens, art, and landscaping aside, there were practical facets with which to deal. The spring 1991 newsletter contains a wish list for the future gift shop cash register, coffee machine,

Rolodex, vacuum cleaner, counters, umbrella holder, bucket and mop, price tags.

And by early June 1992, with the opening only weeks away, activity and emotions seemed to reach a fever pitch, when everything from resurfacing the parking lot to installing "24,000 annuals and garbage cans" was scheduled. The official opening weekend included a preview on June 26, with the public opening the next day. It was a homegrown opening, befitting the Garden and honoring its benefactors. In a note to board members, they were reminded to show up on Saturday morning, June 27, with four dozen cookies each. And "Wear your name tag both days … & wear a smile — IT'S FINALLY HAPPENING!"

ABOVE **The entrance plaza and rill, designed by the Bellevue landscape architecture firm of JGM, greet people on their approach to the Shorts Visitor Center. Visitors are fascinated by the path of the water, which travels just below their feet.** RIGHT **A fundraising effort helped to build the entrance plaza paver by paver. Those interested donated $25 per square.**

GARDEN MANAGEMENT BECOMES FOCUS

A subtle change occurred after the Garden was opened in the summer of 1992. The focus continued on building and creating, but another theme emerged: maintaining. When a garden shifts from the big-picture idea to the reality of continuing the dream, it's really arrived.

Before, during, and after the official opening, fundraising — always a large part of running a public garden — continued, and gardens were built. The NPA Border was expanded in 1994 into a shady section to the south of the original border, the Waterwise Garden opened to help home gardeners understand one of our most precious resources, and the Native and the Alpine Rock gardens became realities after

years of dreams. After several years, the master plan needed revising. As the Garden developed, opportunities arose that were not original to the Garden, but obviously useful and in keeping with the growing Garden and population of visitors.

Gardens never stop changing, which is one of the best and, at the same time, frustrating things we love. Once completed, a garden design and its plants almost inevitably need tweaking or possibly complete renovation. In varying degrees after their opening, gardens began to get that needed refurbishment. The rill, the Waterwise Garden, the Alpine Garden, and the Shorts Ground Cover Garden all took their turns with expansion, revision, or change of some kind. And change came to the master plan, too, in 1996. Iain Robertson looked

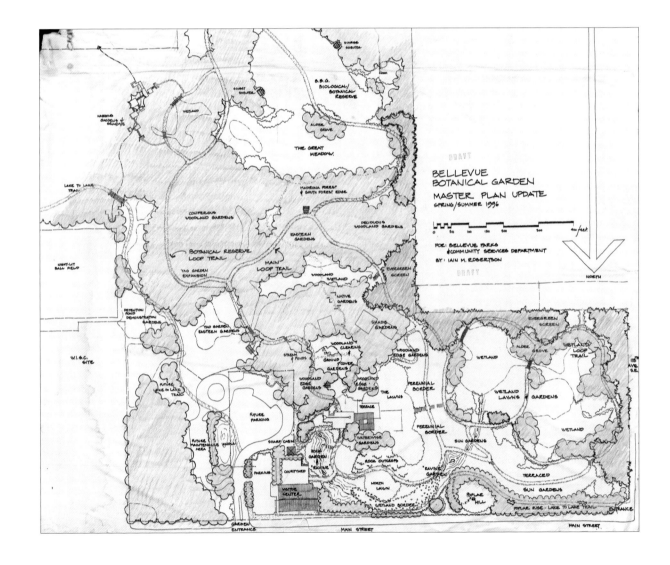

at the original concept and critiqued both it and what had happened since its inception. And then he looked forward.

The patio on the south side of the visitor center was extended in 1993, which affords a view of the grand lawn and border beyond. In addition to the Waterwise Garden, which wraps around the building on the north and west sides, other displays took shape, including large, showy summer pots that bask in the sun against the walls of the building. In beds along the other side of the south patio, a garden display rotates, based on designs from local horticultural students who take turns experimenting with color and form.

The wealth of knowledge and the energy and time that the volunteers have brought to the Garden over the years never

BELOW **Along the north side of the visitor center, rotating displays offer visual interest year-round.** BOTTOM **In 2006, a series of mounds designed by Kelley Hazel, and called** "Stretch," was installed. LEFT **An updated master plan (1996) centered upon interpretation in the Garden, as another way to help educate visitors.**

cease to amaze people. In 2005, 600 volunteers gave more than 18,000 hours of service to the Garden. The Garden continues to be supported by the myriad of people who love parks or gardens or plants. Their examples to follow are the Jewetts, whose vision of a botanical garden helped shape the gift that Cal and Harriet Shorts were willing to leave to the people of Bellevue. Their dedication reflects the Pacific Northwest's high interest in gardening and in public service.

And in plants. Volunteer Eve Sperber went so far as to donate a plant that she herself hybridized while working at the Brooklyn Botanic Garden. *Magnolia* 'Elizabeth', a cross between *M. acuminata* and *M. denudata*, is located at the south end of the lawn and blooms with clear yellow, fragrant flowers in spring. It is a symbol of the dedication and love the volunteers have had for the Garden from the beginning.

Art came to the Garden in a blend of nature and creative display. In August 1993, a basalt sculpture titled "Shaman" by Bainbridge Island artist Will Robinson, with the setting for the piece created by landscape architect Richard VanDeMark, was installed near the visitor center. "Shaman" was followed in 2000 by "The Nature of Sitting" by Pamela Beyette of Seattle. The combination of etched granite and stainless-steel forms a bench that invites quiet contemplation of nature.

The relationship between smooth and rough surfaces is explored in another applied art piece, this time a basalt bench by Barry Namm of Fall City, which was installed in 2006. The fluid lines blend the polished parts of the stone seamlessly with the rough surface. And in 2006, Tom Small's sculpture "Sophia" gave visitors another take on polished basalt. The recumbent figure stands out on the lawn and draws admirers. In 2006, a bronze sculpture of an owl in flight, created by David Maritz, joined the collection.

Sometimes you create gardens, and sometimes gardens are thrust upon you. The Yao Japanese Garden encompasses some of the most interesting aspects of the botanical garden, yet it began life at another Bellevue park — Kelsey Creek Park. Kelsey Creek was the original site for a Japanese garden honoring Yao, Bellevue's sister city, but it turned out to be not the best place, because Kelsey Creek Park flooded frequently in the rainy season.

When Harriet Shorts died in January 1997, the Garden lost one of its benefactors and one of its staunchest supporters. The Society had made Cal and Harriet life members in 1994, and they remained active in the Garden. In May 2000, Cal received a Citizen of the Year award from

RIGHT FROM TOP **Art in the Garden: "Owl's Glare" by David Maritz, located in the Native Discovery Garden; "Shaman" by Will Robinson resides near the visitor center; "The Nature of Sitting" by Pamela Beyette offers visitors contemplation and rest; "Goldiwarts" by Lon Brusselback acts both as art and donation bank; Tom Small's "Sophia" resides in the Waterwise Garden; Barry Namm's basalt bench presents the contrast of a polished surface.**

Tom Kuykendall

All who have touched the Garden have left their legacy, including the Garden's first manager, Tom Kuykendall. Tom's tenure at the Bellevue Botanical Garden ran from 1995 through 2004, but his work with the City's parks began in 1990 and continues. His years as manager were so full that, as Tom puts it, "The whole time I was at the Garden was a big event." The Garden had been open for three years, and many individual gardens were being expanded, developed, or renovated, and Tom had a hand in all of it.

A master's degree from the University of Washington's urban horticulture program, with an emphasis in public garden management, made Tom highly aware of the importance of interpretation in the Garden and of the creative and positive ways that the Garden's educational messages could be translated to visitors.

the International Northwest Parks & Recreation Association.

Gardens are not static like an interior designer's arrangement of furniture. Plants grow, die; soil can shift and with it, rocks. And weather events sometimes take over in the design of a landscape. The Inauguration Day windstorm in January 1993 felled trees and generally made a mess of the Garden, which had been open a mere four months. But the Garden recovered. The City began cleanup, and volunteers pitched in. The landscape was changed from a scene of destruction into a garden again.

In the winter of 1997, it was noted that the ground-cover garden, one of the gardens original to the whole, needed restoration. The knot garden in the parking lot was redesigned. NPA added more to its border display, and the name became plural, the NPA Borders.

If time sped by coming up to the opening of the Garden, it has been a blur since. After Nancy Fonk resigned as curator, Tom Kuykendall took the job now known as garden manager. Tom's tenure, 1995-2004, was full of projects planned and constructed. The Lost Meadow Trail extended the walking opportunities for visitors an additional third of a mile into an area that has stayed much as it grew after early logging in Bellevue. The inter-

est in an alpine display had been high since the Garden's inception, and under Tom's tenure, it finally became a reality in 1997. And Tom was responsible for the renovation of the ground-cover garden, which was finished in two parts, the water feature and enlargement of the planting display, plus the construction of the Tateuchi Pavilion, which gives visitors a viewpoint of the ground-cover hillside.

Tom continues to admire the work of the Society and City for understanding the Garden as an educational resource. Visitors agreed, as over the years average attendance increased from 20,000 annually to about 300,000. They come not only from the neighborhood and the City, but also from all over the world.

The master-plan update, officially

BELOW **The Tateuchi Pavilion, located in the Shorts Ground Cover Garden on the site of Cal's garden shed, affords visitors a place to rest.** LEFT **Volunteers from Starbucks help plant and maintain the Garden. Here, a group installs plants along the Loop trail.**

> "A garden, where one may enter in and forget the whole world, cannot be made in a week, nor a month, nor a year; it must be planned for, waited for, and loved into being."
>
> Chinese proverb

known as "Study and Implementation Guidelines, Summer 1997, prepared by Iain Robertson for City of Bellevue Parks and Community Services Department" and described as an "update to the botanical garden portion of the Wilburton Hill Park Master Plan adopted by City Council in 1989," paid attention to interpretation in the Garden. It stated that "… all gardens should possess underlying educational purposes."

At the Garden's 10th-anniversary celebration, past presidents of the Society were asked for their recollections, and Nancy Davidson Short spent valuable time in conversation with Cal, gathering bits of memory that may have appeared nowhere else. He remembered friends Perry and Jean Johanson, who sparked an interest in Cal and Harriet to grow rhododendrons from seed. He remembered that Wilburton Hill was still country in the 1950s and '60s. Cal

died in March 2003, but not before he had been able to celebrate the Garden's 10th anniversary the previous June.

In addition to the generosity of Cal and Harriet Shorts, others have given to the Garden. Society members and interested residents bought pavers for the plaza and donated money for parts of the Garden. From garden clubs to plant societies, money has been found to supplement the City's budget for the Garden.

Today, the Garden stands again at a threshold, looking back at years of hard work and great joy, and looking forward. The Garden continues to grow, in more ways than one. Membership, which started out between 200 and 300, stands at more than 1,000. And just as plants mature, so do gardens. In March 2006, 17 acres were added for a total of 53. The new land is adjacent to the Lost Meadow and doubles the area left as a nature reserve.

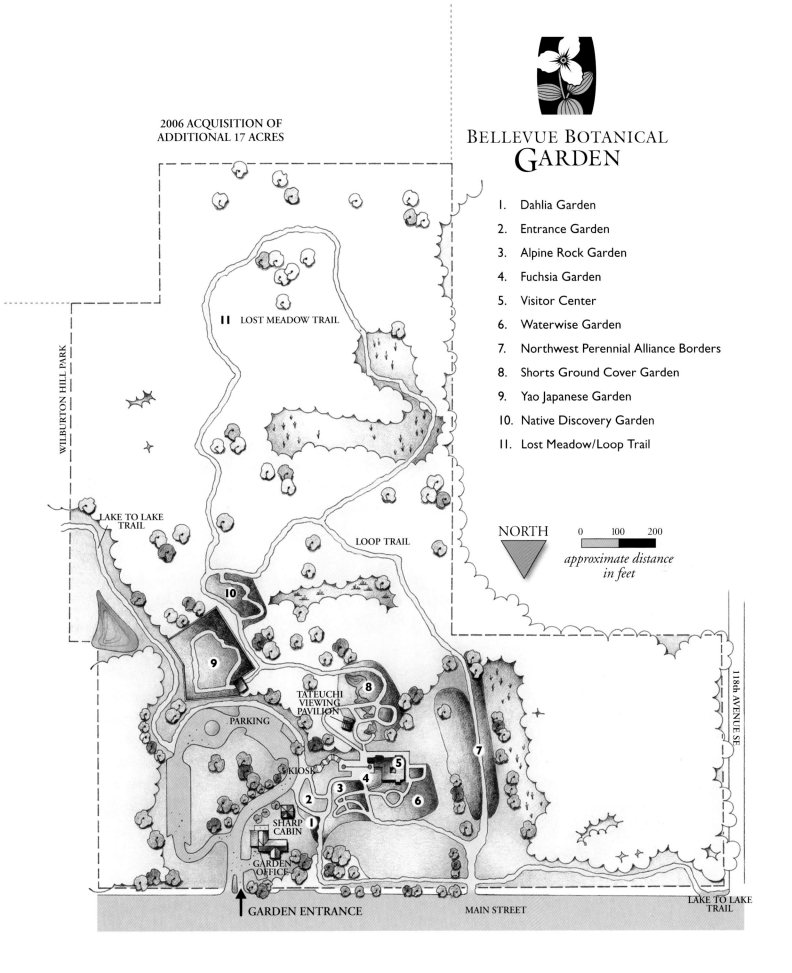

2006 ACQUISITION OF
ADDITIONAL 17 ACRES

BELLEVUE BOTANICAL
GARDEN

1. Dahlia Garden
2. Entrance Garden
3. Alpine Rock Garden
4. Fuchsia Garden
5. Visitor Center
6. Waterwise Garden
7. Northwest Perennial Alliance Borders
8. Shorts Ground Cover Garden
9. Yao Japanese Garden
10. Native Discovery Garden
11. Lost Meadow/Loop Trail

11 LOST MEADOW TRAIL

WILBURTON HILL PARK

LAKE TO LAKE TRAIL

LOOP TRAIL

NORTH

0   100   200
approximate distance
in feet

10

9

TATEUCHI
VIEWING
PAVILION

8

PARKING

KIOSK

5

4

3

2

7

6

118th AVENUE SE

SHARP
CABIN

1

GARDEN
OFFICE

GARDEN ENTRANCE   MAIN STREET   LAKE TO LAKE
TRAIL

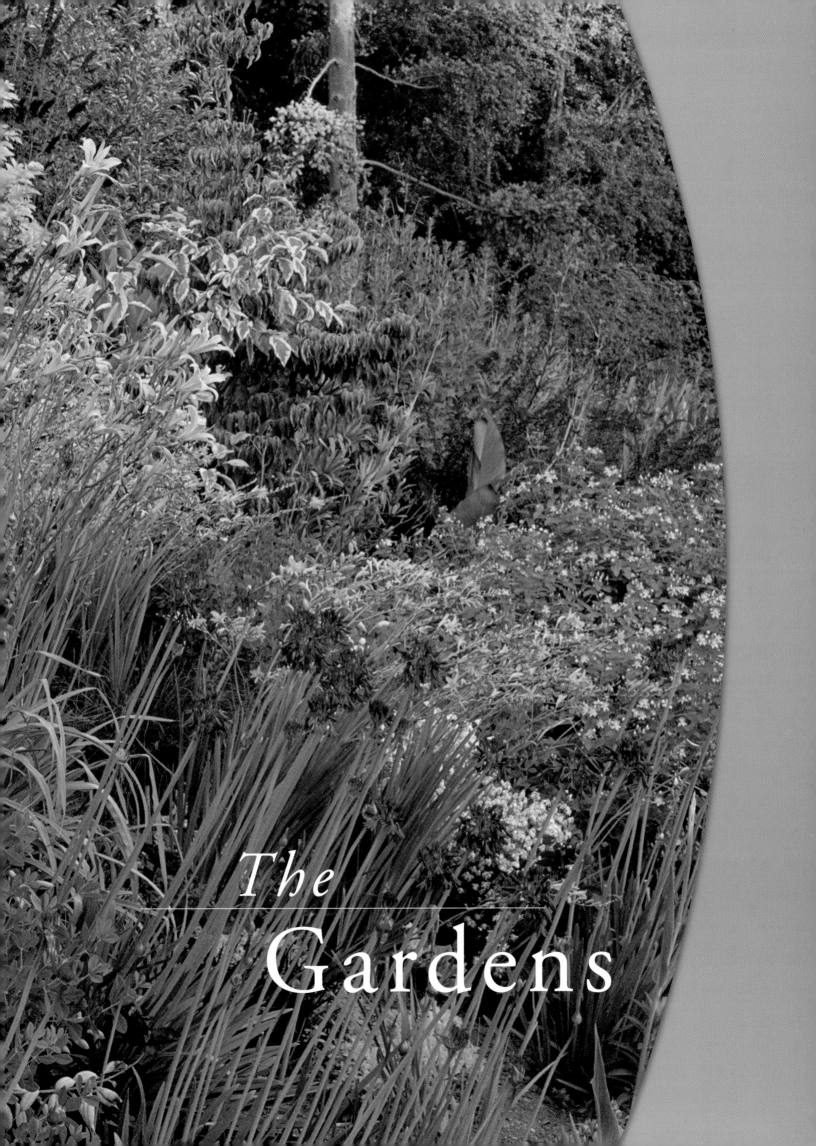

The
Gardens

The Gardens

"It far exceeded my expectations. I never dreamed they'd create the place they did, with all the gardens such as the perennial border." Lee Springgate

The Bellevue Botanical Garden comprises a wide variety of gardens. Although each is distinctive in its design, plant selection, and size, together they make up a wealth of information for gardeners seeking to learn what best grows in our Pacific Northwest climate. But the gardens are more than useful educational displays for local gardeners; they are contemplative stroll gardens, flamboyant with color and form,

ABOVE **The Northwest Perennial Alliance Borders were designed, planted, and have been maintained by volunteers for all the 15 years that they have been in existence.**

highlighting the beauty in a variety of environments. Figuratively and literally, these gardens are open to the world. The individual gardens represent the inspiration and hard work of many groups, and the cooperation among all involved is vital to the success of each display as well as the success of the Garden as a whole. In each case where appropriate, the City and the sponsoring organization have reached an agreement about all aspects of the display, from the size to how the Garden will be maintained.

Anyone who has worked in one of the gardens knows that gardeners love to know the names of plants. As part of the Society's outreach, a plant-collection database was created that can be accessed from both the Society's Web site (www.bellevuebotanical.org) and the City's Web site (www.cityofbellevue.net). The goal is to have all plants in all the gardens listed in the database. Plants can be searched by scientific or common name, location in the Garden, or plant characteristics. The information returned includes an ever-growing library of photos.

The organizations that have developed and maintain the individual display gardens represent a vital partnership with the City, reached by a mutual agreement. The City relies on them to keep up their part of the bargain. Volunteers serve as workers in all the displays.

The Society's online plant database is a growing component. Photos and cultural information for plants in all the gardens are being added continually. CURRENT INCLUSIONS FROM THE TOP *Clematis heracleifolia* **(shrub clematis) in the Entrance Garden and the NPA Borders;** *Sempervivum* **'Packard-** **ian' in the Alpine Garden;** *Hypericum androsaemum* **'Glacier' (syn.** *Hypericum* × *inodorum* **'Glacier') in the Waterwise Garden;** *Lilium* **'Pink Perfection'** RIGHT **In early summer, the large flower heads of** *Allium* **'Globemaster' show up well against the acid-yellow foliage of** *Berberis thunbergii* **'Aurea'.**

NORTHWEST PERENNIAL ALLIANCE BORDERS

Fashions may fade, only to return years later to embarrass the formerly fashion-conscious, but color never goes out of style. When Charles Price and Glenn Withey approached the Bellevue Botanical Garden Society and the City to propose including a large mixed border of perennials and shrubs that would be designed, planted, and maintained by members of the Northwest Perennial Alliance — Western Washington's hardy plant society — hardly anyone knew what was in store.

Certainly they never dreamed that the border would gain international recognition, be photographed constantly, and appear in several national garden magazines

ABOVE **A volunteer studies the layout of what will become the NPA Border.** BELOW **NPA volunteers participate in work parties at least twice a month, and students from Edmonds Community College take classes in border maintenance.** OPPOSITE **The wiry stems of a cultivar of *Clematis montana*, which bloom in early summer, scramble over a fence here in the NPA Borders.**

— more than once. Mostly, the Society and the City were concerned that the project was a bit too ambitious for the group and the designers — Glenn, Charles, Bob Lilly, and Carrie Becker — and that the promised volunteer help would fade away as time wore on.

Now, 15 years later, no one would believe that. The NPA Borders — for now there is more than one — stand as a shining example of hard work and commitment, in addition to design and a love of plants. The original border, which was installed in 1992, was followed soon after by the shade border, located directly to the south. In 1995, the west border was installed on the other side of the path. The total garden space runs to about 25,000 square feet.

For the past 15 years, volunteers have gathered twice a month to help maintain the borders. Yearly volunteer time in the borders is estimated to be more than 1,500 hours. Students work in the borders, too. Since 1994, four quarters a year, Carrie Becker has taught a border-maintenance class through the environmental horticulture program at Edmonds Community College.

The site for the original border lay across the lawn from the visitor center. Standing on the patio, the border looks long, but there is no way to tell how deep it is, or that it drops down a steep incline. There's no visual cue that another border exists on the other side of the lower trail, and only a peek of the shade border on the south end can be seen. The view from the

RIGHT **Every season has its highlights in the NPA Borders** FROM TOP **The spring blooms of** *Fritillaria meleagris* **(checker lily); summer red of** *Astilbe* × *arendsii* **'Fanal'; warm autumn tones of** *Rudbeckia fulgida* **var.** *sullivantii* **'Goldsturm'; winter, when hellebores rule, including many selections of** *Helleborus* × *hybridus.*

terrace is impressive, but it is only the tip of the iceberg, and when visitors take in the whole, they are astounded.

The design takes its cue from the traditional style of English border, but is definitely a Northwest take on the subject. The original border is half as long as a football field with paths that cut through the spine, although in the height of summer, these paths narrow considerably. Along the "spine" grow large shrubs, such as *Sambucus nigra* (elderberry; cultivars include 'Guincho Purple'), and trees, including *Liriodendron tulipifera* 'Aureomarginatum' (variegated tulip tree). Those give structure to the garden when the herbaceous plants die back in winter and lend support to various clematis and other vines that grow throughout the borders.

The color scheme is in broad swaths and grouped into sections. From the visitor center, three sections can be seen: pink; cerise and gold; and variegated and saturated. On the gravel path below, the other color sections can be seen: the hot border; yellow, black, and blue section; and salmon, apricot, lavender, and blue section. The color sections often relate to particular times of the year, especially the hot border in August and September. Deep purples come from the many kinds of *Berberis*, including *B. thunbergii f. atropurpurea* 'Helmond Pillar', an upright selection that has matured to show gardeners the shrub can grow as wide as it is high — to about 5 feet. Other dark colors come from the shrub *Physocarpus opulifolius* 'Diablo', a dark-leaved ninebark. Warm red and orange tones show up in many different cultivars of *Hemerocallis* (daylily) and in cherry-colored *Penstemon* and golden *Rudbeckia fulgida* var. *sullivantii* 'Goldsturm'.

Salvias, penstemon, hardy fuchsias, and other summer bloomers combine to create a great place to view hummingbirds. At times, the hummingbird activity is so high that you get the feeling you have invaded their personal airspace.

Although plant lists for the garden exist, NPA workers urge gardeners to use the borders as an example. It's never been about particular plants but the ability to see color, form, and sequence, and then choose from what may seem like an unending supply of great garden plants. The advice is choose and plant well.

Within each of the borders, layering of plants from the ground up shows visitors that more plants mean a more impressive display. From creeping ground covers such as *Lysimachia nummularia* 'Aurea' (golden creeping jenny) and *Acaena* (New Zealand

burr) to *Ajuga* (bugleweed) and *Stachys byzantina* (lamb's ears), the ground is indeed coated with plants.

And reseeding plants are not necessarily disposed of; in fact, some, such as *Tanacetum parthenium* (feverfew) are cherished — or at least tolerated — for their tenacity and timing, often blooming over long periods or in tough times.

High summer may be a big draw to the borders, including the shade border with its cool blue hydrangeas, but frequent visitors find that there's a show at any time of the year. In fall, as herbaceous perennials are dying back, shrubs such as the deciduous *Berberis* take on bright shades of orange and red, echoed in the shade border by several *Hamamelis* (witch hazel). Any quiet garden time is soon taken over with a huge

ABOVE **In the hot section, daylilies mix with the oranges of *Crocosmia* 'Lucifer', *Kniphofia* 'Bressingham Comet', and the deep purple of *Berberis thunbergii* 'Rose Glow' and 'Helmond Pillar'.**

BELOW ***Lysimachia nummularia* 'Aurea' (golden creeping jenny) and *Ajuga reptans* 'Catlin's Giant'** in the hot section. FAR LEFT TOP **In the cerise-and-gold section, *Catalpa bignonioides* 'Aurea' (golden Indian bean tree) with *Geranium psilostemon* and the shrub rose 'Cerise Bouquet'.**

FAR LEFT BOTTOM **At the south end, pink-and-green *Tulipa* 'Greenland' brightens spring.**

ABOVE **Northwest Perennial Alliance volunteers work year-round in the Borders. The result of winter mulch applications can be seen in the healthy and robust growth of all the plants.**

RIGHT **Ornamental grasses seem to flow down the hill like water in the Borders. Here, several *Miscanthus sinensis* 'Morning Light' (maiden grass) surround a tawny clump of *Stipa tenuissima* (syn. *Nasella tenuissima*, Mexican feather grass).**

display of *Helleborus × hybridus* (Lenten rose), which can start blooming before Christmas. The bulb show picks up with tens of thousands of crocuses, daffodils, and species tulips.

It may seem as if there is no time for anyone to get into the garden for maintenance, but hardy NPA volunteers spend many hours a month all year long. In winter, it is time to spread the mulch — more than 80 cubic yards of dairy manure. Volunteers apply it by bucketfuls, often on top of herbaceous perennials that have been cut back. Gardeners have found that the perennials have no trouble growing through the light, fluffy organic material come spring.

The designers found challenges in the borders just as gardeners find challenges at home — only, of course, on a larger scale.

BELOW **The mature Borders allow visitors to see what plants will look like after several years. An example is the upright shrub** *Berberis thunbergii* **'Helmond Pillar', which begins life as a narrow form, but eventually grows 5 feet wide.** TOP RIGHT *Hamamelis* × *intermedia* **'Diane'.** BOTTOM RIGHT *Phytolacca americana,* **a North American native, produces black fruit that is much loved by visiting cedar waxwings.**

Much of the land is heavy clay soil, and during the first planting, volunteers were surprised to discover a stream running down one part of the slope. Plant ideas were shifted, and perennials that grow well in heavy, wet soil were put there.

Remnants of Cal and Harriet's orchard still exist in the borders; two old apple trees in the original border and one on the west side give the garden a feeling of age. And the apples are tasty, too.

Like life, the Borders have matured, and over the years, some editing was necessary. It still is. And, as the years progress, watering techniques have changed. Original soaker hoses were replaced with a kind of emitter system, which helps put the water directly where it's needed. Plants change, and NPA knew early on that keep-

ing such a garden labeled would be impossible. They have discovered that labels tend either to walk away or the labels draw visitors into the border where no path exists. To save plants, the group makes handouts available that identify plants by season and section.

Seasonal standouts in the borders bring repeated questions to the volunteers on duty during the year. What is that tall plant with the black berries? *Phytolacca americana* (American pokeweed) grows up to 8 feet high, which is impressive enough, but in late summer, black fruit develops from the pinkish flowers. Carrie Becker sees cedar waxwings in the garden feasting on the berries.

Fragrance is a strong favorite in the garden. In winter, gardeners follow their noses to the semievergreen *Lonicera fragrantissima*, a shrubby honeysuckle with small but potent creamy white flowers, and to *Edgeworthia chrysantha*, a deciduous shrub known not only for its heady perfume, but also the silvery flower buds on bare stems. Gardeners tend to walk straight to the shrubs for a closer inspection, even if it is through the border. Carrie Becker and Bob Lilly have heard them referred to as admiration paths.

The admiration of visitors for the borders extends far beyond one path, of course. Photographers, horticulturists, gardeners, and casual visitors all are impressed with the magnificent display.

BELOW **Opening ceremonies in the Yao Garden in October 1994 included a performance, visiting dignitaries, and a chance for the public to experience a new landscape.**

RIGHT **Color in the Yao Japanese Garden often comes not just from flowers, but also from foliage, as seen here with a red-leaved Japanese maple (Acer palmatum).**

The Bellevue Botanical Garden inherited the Yao Japanese Garden when it was moved from its first home at Kelsey Creek Park. The garden honored Bellevue's Japanese sister city, Yao, which is directly east of Osaka City. The garden in Kelsey Creek was established in 1971 to honor that connection, but Kelsey Creek includes wetlands, and the garden area was prone to flooding — not the best circumstances for a Japanese-style garden. And so the Bellevue Botanical Garden inherited both the plants and the idea of a garden linked to a sister city.

In 1992, the garden was relocated to the Bellevue Botanical Garden. The City took on the difficult task of moving 30- to 40-foot-high trees from Kelsey Creek Park to the garden. The new, large trees gave the garden an immediate look of establishment. But the design of a Japanese garden is more than a collection of trees. The new garden site, southeast of the Shorts Visitor Center, was dedicated in October 1992, when officials from Yao were visiting Bellevue, but the completed garden was not dedicated until October 1994.

To create a garden worthy of the site and its reason for being, the talents of landscape architect Robert Murase were called upon. Murase was well-known for being able to blend Japanese design into Northwest settings. The garden is the perfect combination of beauty and function and represents a Northwest interpretation of Japanese garden design. The Japanese elements that Murase used included borrowing views, using plants for texture and form, placing stone, offering places to rest and contemplate, and incorporating water.

On approach, the visitor may note

ABOVE **Japanese garden design relies on contrasting textures of leaves.** TOP **The Yao Garden gate shows the influence of the 16th-century style** **Sukiya, or teahouse, and uses traditional Japanese joinery.** RIGHT **Seasonal displays bring the garden to life in any month.**

that the plantings outside the fence subtly change from the woodsy Native Discovery Garden to Asian-inspired and design-driven choices. Northwest natives such as *Asarum caudatum* (wild ginger) and *Adiantum pedatum* (maidenhair fern) begin to mix with fall-blooming *Camellia sasanqua* 'Hana Jiman' and *Corylopsis pauciflora* (buttercup winterhazel). The choices are careful and placement is important, helping to show off branching structure as well as flowers. And foliage increases in importance. The gray, dusty indumentum of *Rhododendron* 'Golfer' draws the eye. Before passing through the gates, visitors note that only traditional building methods were used.

The design of the gate is derivative of the Sukiya, or teahouse, type from 16th-century Japan. Its simple and elegant lines show off the natural material *(Chamaecyparis lawsoniana)* that was used. The exposed roof and ceiling boards and door panels are made from *Thuja plicata* (Western red cedar), and they are fastened with wedged and pegged mortise and tenon joinery, using traditional Japanese building methods. Japanese hand tools were used, including finishing the gate with a hand plane, not sandpaper. Dale Brotherton, of the Takumi Co., created the gate.

Through the gate, the visitor strolls through the garden along the main path, with views opening and closing along the way. Seasonal displays keep the garden fresh throughout the year. The stark visual image of *Acer davidii* (stripebark maple) against evergreens in winter, candelabra

primroses along the streamside in late spring, and the quiet summer scene punctuated by late-flowering *Hydrangea paniculata* 'Angel's Blush' (syn. 'Ruby') all add to year-round pleasure.

Elements of stone gain importance in a Japanese garden. In the Yao Garden, three stone lanterns, which were a gift from the City of Yao, and an antique stone basin are placed around the garden to help slow the visitor's step, encouraging contemplation. One hundred tons of Columbia Basin basalt were brought into and placed around the garden. Japanese garden design highlights indigenous use of materials, and the rocks in the Yao Garden are well-suited to their surroundings. Large rocks carefully placed give the garden an ancient feel. Some are for viewing only, but others are

Azaleas are a highlight in spring and show off well against a foliar backdrop.

In late spring and early summer, candelabra primroses fill the edges of the streambed.

ABOVE **One hundred tons of Columbia Basin basalt were used in the garden. Japanese garden design emphasizes the use of local materials. The streambed in the Yao Garden is actually part of a storm-water retention system.** RIGHT **Large flat stones are used by many visitors as benches.**

ABOVE **The winding path through the Japanese garden provides visitors with a new scene at every turn.** RIGHT **The delicate layer of autumn leaves on stone reveals just one of the many quiet scenes of beauty.**

seating areas, and it does not take visitors more than a few visits to pick a favorite rock and place to rest.

When inside the quiet garden, it can be a surprise to realize that the space runs along part of the parking lot. The enclosing fence, along with a well-planted border on both sides of it, screens out any distractions, and the Yao Garden becomes what it is intended to be—a respite, a quiet moment in a busy world.

Another element of both beauty and the function is the large pond. The Yao Garden water feature acts as a storm-water retention site. In 1998, the north side of the garden was renovated, drain lines installed, and raised beds added. During the rainy season, the pond can be full, but even during the dry weeks of summer, the idea of water is present in the way the rocks were placed — as if they themselves were the flowing water.

Throughout its life, the Yao Garden has benefited from the talents of several companies that constructed and landscaped the display. Olympic Tree Service moved the large trees from Kelsey Creek, Star Masonry helped set rocks, noted Japanese instructor and author Patricia Swerda and the Yao Sister City Association oversaw the project, and Yorozu Gardening planted.

The efforts of many and the blend of Japanese and Northwest garden styles helped to create a smooth, comforting, and peaceful garden that draws visitors through its gates time and time again.

SHORTS GROUND COVER GARDEN

The Shorts Ground Cover Garden has had at once a checkered and celebrated history. Its story is one of triumph, disaster, then triumph again. It is a garden that is both useful and beautiful and reveals itself a little at a time to visitors who walk on its paths.

First, there was a small mountain stream that Cal built out behind the house. He used rocks that he and Harriet gathered on their weekly mountain walks. It was a place where they could sit and eat their meals. Later, when the Garden was being planned, the idea of a ground-cover garden in that area was brought up. The Society board discussed the concept and entertained plans as early as 1991.

Harriet chose landscape designer Pat Roome to create the garden. Pat talked with Cal and Harriet Shorts about what they wanted the garden to become, in addition to what was possible on the site. Harriet envisioned a garden full of sun-loving ground covers, but the site held the usual tall evergreens.

Pat took them down to meet Ione and Emmott Chase, whose woodland garden in Orting took advantage of similar conditions. Harriet loved the Chase Garden, now part of the Garden Conservancy, and she and Cal gave generously to see the ground-cover garden completed.

The display featured shade-loving plants that suited the situation under the tall trees. It was designed "to capture the essence of the Chase Garden in Orting," Pat

explained to the board. Lynn Sonneman added a tumbling mountain stream to Cal's original water pump, and Pat Roome's overall ground cover-garden design was installed.

It took one big windstorm to turn the shady ground-cover garden into the full-sun site that Harriet originally had wanted. The Inauguration Day windstorm of January 20, 1993, took out most of the large conifers that created the shade for the garden. Cleanup ensued, but it was clear that eventually the garden would need to be remade.

Today's ground-cover garden is the result of a two-part renovation. First, the water feature was entirely rebuilt to correct drainage problems and to enlarge it. Next, the new landscaping was installed. And a teahouse-style building, which serves as a

ABOVE **The Inauguration Day windstorm in 1993 took out many trees in the Garden, including several conifers in the Ground Cover Garden. It turned from a shady site to full sun, overnight.** BELOW **Water cascades down the hillside and** past the plantings of trees, shrubs, and perennials that add variety to the ground-cover demonstration. LEFT **The Tateuchi Pavilion, built on the site of Cal's garden shed, occupies a prime viewing place in the ground-cover garden.**

viewing platform for the garden, was designed by Hoshide-Williams Architects and funded by the Atsuhiko and Ina Goodwin Tateuchi Foundation.

The garden water feature was designed by landscape architect Richard VanDeMark and built by Turnstone Construction. The garden is larger than the original, and the new water element takes full advantage of the space and the slope that starts just behind the visitor center. A stop at either the top or bottom of the waterfall affords visitors the opportunity to stop and contemplate the gift Cal and Harriet left. Wide benches and a boardwalk in the lower part of the garden allow time to stop and read the interpretive boards that pay tribute to their generosity.

The Portico Group, with Kate Day as lead designer, created the garden design. In addition to installation by Turnstone, landscape designer Terry Welch gave advice. When it came time to plant, city workers — and volunteers, of course — pitched in to get the job done.

Enlarging the Shorts Ground Cover Garden made room not just for more plants, but also to take visitors on a longer journey. Paths meander back and forth, bridges cross the water, and steps lead to unexpected discoveries. One discovery, especially delightful for children, is Cal and Harriet's old root cellar, which looks for all the world like the door to a hobbit hole.

From the bottom of the garden looking up, it is not possible to see the entire water feature. Shrubs, such as the winter-flowering *Mahonia* × *media* 'Underway',

help to disguise the entire garden. But standing at the source of the waterfall, with the visitor center at your back, you can watch the water as it progresses from each pool and over each fall. The garden holds constant surprises.

Of course, the plants within the garden help gardeners learn more about ground covers — that lowest of layers in a layered garden. Trees such as *Metasequoia glyptostroboides* 'Gold Rush' (dawn redwood) begin to cast some shade over ground covers such as *Acorus gramineus* 'Pusillus'.

Although the garden lies near the visitor center just to the south, it feels as if it is a place unto itself.

BELOW **Education, on signs and in handouts, is key in the Waterwise Garden.** BOTTOM **The hot, sunny section of the Waterwise Garden offers gardeners ideas for low-water-** use practices, including *Akebia* and grapes grown on the arbor. RIGHT **Path materials demonstrated, along with examples of plants that prefer a hot, full-sun aspect.**

The Waterwise Garden was dedicated May 8, 1994, in a successful effort to educate gardeners and homeowners in smart ways to use water, one of our most precious resources, to choose and place plants, and to build healthy soil that benefits both the home garden and the environment. It was funded by the City and Bellevue Utilities and designed by Stenn Design, Northwest garden designers skilled and knowledgeable about the unique quality of the climate and the region's resources.

Outside the maritime Pacific Northwest, most people think it rains all the time here, but residents know better. The cool Mediterranean climate, wet winters, and dry summers mean that gardeners must

choose, locate, and maintain their gardens knowing which plants need supplemental water in the summer and which don't. That, coupled with rapid population growth in the Northwest, means that there are more people sharing the same amount of water. The idea of a garden that displays how to use low amounts of water in the garden, a concept that was brought up at the beginning of planning for the BBG, was ahead of its time. It now is exemplary in its ability to show home gardeners how to do it.

The garden was designed by Howard and Jil Stenn. Since its inception, Patricia Burgess, resource conservation program administrator with the City of Bellevue, has supervised the project and maintenance, including coordinating all the volunteers who

work to keep up the garden. The garden was purposely situated around the visitor center so that the space was grounded as a home garden. Both shady and sunny aspects are used — as well as edges of part or filtered sun. As typical in the Northwest, tall native conifers cast shade and soak up available water. The sunny garden offers ideas for a Mediterranean-style terrace garden, where rosemary and sage vie for a place with ornamentals. But the shade garden tackles real problems that many gardeners face.

Gardeners are surprised to find so many plants that grow well in dry shade, yet here they are. Broadleaf evergreens, such as *Lonicera pileata* (privet honeysuckle) and *Sarcococca hookeriana* var. *humilis* and *S. ruscifolia* (sweet box), hold year-round presence and show how to use tall

ABOVE **Layers of plantings exhibit the beauty of a garden with an eye toward conservation. Here, a ground cover of *Epimedium* × *cantabrigiense* (apricot bishop's hat) is layered with *Cornus alba* 'Elegantissima' (Tartarian dogwood).** RIGHT **Homeowners get ideas from the Waterwise Garden's practical use of plants and hardscape.** FAR RIGHT

FROM TOP **Wine-red tulips combine with a purple-leaved Heuchera for a spring show. *Hemerocallis* 'Frans Hals' adds fire to a summer display. In autumn, *Hydrangea quercifolia* (oakleaf hydrangea) shows its burgundy tones. The winter display of catkins on *Garrya* × *issaquahensis* (coast silk tassel) puts on a good show.**

ground covers. Deciduous shrubs, including *Hydrangea quercifolia* (oakleaf hydrangea) and *Physocarpus opulifolius* 'Dart's Gold', play their roles in flower and foliage.

Such a variety of perennials grows in the shade garden that gardeners would be hard-pressed to try to include them all at home. Several colorful-leaved cultivars of *Heuchera* (coral bells) and hardy geraniums, such as *Geranium macrorrhizum* (evergreen geranium) and *G. phaeum* (mourning widow), fill in a lower layer of interest.

Good use is made of all situations. A sunny kitchen garden displays the use of herbs such as *Rosmarinus officinalis* (rosemary) and *Salvia officinalis* 'Icterina', the variegated culinary sage. Mixed in with the grapes and lavender are ornamentals that prefer a hot site — *Solidago* 'Golden Fleece', *Co-*

tinus coggygria 'Royal Purple' (purple smoke tree) and *Ceanothus* 'Julia Phelps' (California lilac). The emphasis changes and plants go in and out of flower through the year, but there is always something happening.

In winter, evergreen shrubs, includ-

Patricia Burgess

Education is key to the work that Patricia Burgess has accomplished for the Garden. Patricia, who works for Bellevue Utilities, started the Living Lab program at the Garden in 1994. The program brings schoolchildren from kindergarten through fifth grade into the Garden, through its lessons and activities. But Patricia doesn't stop at educating children; she educates adult gardeners, too. As resource conservation program administrator, she is responsible for the Waterwise Garden. Here, both the avid gardener and the casual visitor are exposed to good garden practices. Both design and plant choice exhibit how to garden in harmony with our environment, by judicious use of water and well-chosen placement of plants. The Waterwise Garden is on a scale that home gardeners can understand, and Patricia sees that as a great strength of the demonstration. But visitors know that it's not just the solid practicality of the garden that helps educate, but also its beauty.

ing variegated selections such as *Elaeagnus pungens* 'Maculata' and *E.* × *ebbingei* 'Gilt Edge', light up dark days, whereas early flowers from the high ground cover *Epimedium* (bishop's cap) herald spring to come. And in all seasons, Northwest natives including *Vaccinium ovatum* (evergreen huckleberry) can be admired.

But, as elsewhere, the garden has not remained static. The loss of a few trees over the years prompted changes in planting, but Patricia and her workers, who are often on hand to answer questions from visitors, always consider these occasions opportunities to improve on the message they deliver. It's a part of the mission of the Bellevue Utilities' water-conservation program, which funded the display. And the mission is fulfilled continually — the garden can

be used both as an interesting and attractive place to visit and, at the same time, as a shining example that teaches Bellevue residents and all visitors how to use our precious resources.

ABOVE **Two *Amelanchier* × *grandiflora* 'Autumn Brilliance' (serviceberry) flank the entrance to the Waterwise Garden, showing colorful fall foliage. A year-round display includes small white flowers in spring and a dusting of snow in winter.**

LEFT **The bright yellow-green foliage of *Robinia pseudoacacia* 'Frisia' (golden black locust) brightens the shady section, while below, *Acanthus spinosus* (bear's breech) and *Anemone* × *hybrida* 'Honorine Jobert' (Japanese anemone) bloom.**

"I've rarely seen a group of volunteers with an end product of that quality."

ENTRANCE GARDEN

First impressions are important, and the Entrance Garden impresses visitors immediately with the plant combinations and the skillful use of topography. The garden can be entered two ways, but both show off the features of the Paisley Bed, the dahlia display, and the slope of the grass bed. From high summer through fall, visitors who take the path that leads past the Sharp cabin get a close look at the dahlia display, in existence since 1993. It is planted and maintained every year by members of the Puget Sound Dahlia Association.

This upper path, suitable for wheelchairs, lets visitors stroll around the Paisley Bed, named for the shape of the planting area. This small display is chock-full

ABOVE **Ornamental grasses in the Entrance Garden give the impression of water falling down the slope.** TOP **An aerial view of the ornamental grass bed when it was first planted shows the swirl-** ing effect. LEFT **Each year, the Dahlia Garden is planted and maintained by the Puget Sound Dahlia Association.**

of planting ideas; it was adapted from a design project created by students in Don Marshall's environmental horticulture program at Lake Washington Technical College in Kirkland.

Throughout summer, the entrance garden is abuzz with bees first attending *Ceanothus* × *pallidus* 'Marie Simon' (California lilac) and then fragrant *Clethra alnifolia* (summersweet). Summer perennials fill in, including *Potentilla nepalensis* 'Miss Willmott', with its pink-red flowers, and the blue daisies of *Aster* × *frikartii* 'Mönch'.

But early and later visitors receive their own rewards: In February, rose-purple blossoms coat the branches of *Cercis chinensis* (Chinese redbud), May brings the white handkerchief blooms of *Davidia involucrata*, and late in the year, *Parrotia*

ABOVE **The Sharp Cabin is located next to the Entrance Garden.** TOP **Mature rhododendrons greet visitors at the top of the steps leading to the entrance plaza.**

persica (Persian ironwood) bursts into flaming colors.

The approach takes the visitor past the top of the Alpine Rock Garden, giving them a taste of the beauty that lives in harsh environments. But many other visitors enter the garden from the parking lot and walk up the steps to the plaza. This path gives them a view up the slope of ornamental grasses designed by landscape architect Sally Promer Nichols.

Sally created visual movement and accentuated the slope by using grasses with a soft, flowing texture. Bunches of the blond *Stipa tenuissima* (Mexican feather grass) seem to flow and sway and are surrounded by ever-widening sweeps of other grasses, including Japanese blood grass, *Imperata cylindrica* 'Rubra' (syn. 'Red Baron'); *Festuca glauca* 'Elijah Blue' (blue fescue); and *Ophiopogon planiscapus* 'Nigrescens' (black mondo grass). Those are planted in a serpentine fashion to fill in the unusually shaped space. At the top of the slope, Sally integrated the bed on either side of the path by overlapping the sweep of grasses.

From either direction, the visitor emerges at the top of the walk onto the entrance plaza and rill. The visitor has arrived.

FROM TOP **A show of early-flowering *Narcissus* greets visitors; the soft pink flowers of *Ceanothus* × *pallidus* 'Marie Simon' in early summer; in fall, *Parrotia persica* (Persian ironwood) bursts into color.**

ABOVE **High Cascade granite was used to form much of the Alpine Garden.** TOP **At the dedication of the Alpine Rock Garden, Nell Scott is congratulated for her fundraising work.** RIGHT **Low-growing and hummocky plants are well-suited to the harsh alpine environment, as demonstrated in the display garden.**

Talk of an alpine garden ran throughout the early years before the Garden opened — and after, too. But the effort took a few years and was made possible by the fundraising work of Nell Scott. The Garden was dedicated on Mother's Day, May 11, 1997. The garden lies just northeast of the Shorts Visitor Center.

Iain Robertson's original 1989 drawing of what the garden might include made room for an alpine display, and the Society began to make the garden a reality. But, as with other parts of the garden, funding was a main concern. Scott, longtime board member and president of the Society when the garden opened in 1992, spearheaded the fundraising effort and was able to present the City with the money for the Alpine Rock Garden.

Landscape designer Micheal Moshier, who was a member of the board and worked on the alpine display for years, created the design for the garden and helped install the work with the help of volunteers.

Perhaps the work that went into installing the garden reflects the type of garden it is. The alpine garden exhibits the harsh environment faced by plants living around or above timberline. Extremes of temperature, water, and soil are common, and the plants that grow well there have adapted to the situation.

Around the edges of the garden is the area of horticultural interest. The plantings here are softer and give visitors ideas of what might grow in a home garden in or along a rockery. Small spring-flowering shrubs, such as *Rhododendron* 'Ramapo', with violet-blue flowers; *R*. 'Ginny Gee', with icy-pink trusses; and bright pink

R. 'Wigeon' brighten up the spring and provide a low evergreen throughout the year.

Alpine plants must conserve energy and resources, and so are often found as low-growing, hummocky forms, such as *Armeria maritima* (thrift), also found hunkered down on seaside bluffs, and *Phlox diffusa* (creeping phlox). Both plants are represented in the alpine display by cultivars: the dark-leaved thrift 'Rubrifolia' and the rich pink phlox 'Goat Rocks Pink'.

Drainage is key in an alpine garden, because the plants grow best in a rock mixture that lets water slide by their roots. The soil mix, which was dug in to a depth of up to 24 inches, was made up of three-eighths-inch washed and screened crushed rock (50 percent), pumice (20 percent), and compost (30 percent). High Cascade granite was used in much of the garden, with rounder stones of Bandera granite.

Small evergreens nestle into the rocky outcroppings, including *Tsuga mertensiana* (mountain hemlock), a Northwest native, and one of its cultivars, the low-growing 'Elizabeth'. The evergreens not only add interest when other plants are out of flower, but also act as a green backdrop when blooms do appear.

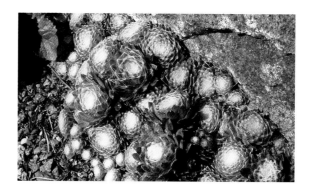

The dense, miniature form of *Pinus strobus* 'Greg's Witches Broom' (a form of Eastern white pine), bronze-tinted *Chamaecyparis obtusa* 'Pygmaea Aurescens', and *Picea sitchensis* 'Nana', a dwarf Sitka spruce, dot the landscape.

The garden was renovated in 2000, the design by Kate Day from the Portico Group and with Micheal Moshier, in order to expand the garden and improve both interpretation and flow for visitors. Signage explains the unique environment of an alpine garden, and paths now lead visitors through and out of the display in a loop.

The Alpine Rock Garden is the perfect mountain getaway that requires little climbing experience.

LEFT **Crimson-red with a white center,** *Primula auricula* **'Argus' is small but exquisite.** ABOVE *Pulsatilla vulgaris* **(pasqueflower) grows well against the warm stone in the Alpine Rock Garden.**

ABOVE **Gray squirrels make themselves at home in the Garden.** RIGHT **Interpretive signs explain to visitors what an alpine garden is and the conditions that suit alpine plants.** BELOW **High Cascade granite was used in much of the Alpine Rock Garden.**

BELOW **Visitors who stop to check out directions to other displays are delighted to see hummingbirds zipping through the Fuchsia Garden.**

RIGHT **The list of fuchsias in the display is never the same from year to year.**

FUCHSIA GARDEN

For months on end in the summer and into autumn, hummingbirds put on a show near the entrance to the visitor center, as they attend to the blossoms in the fuchsia garden. The Eastside Fuchsia Society planned, planted, and has maintained the garden since it opened in June 1992. Ollie de Graaf and Harry King had the first shovels in their hands. At 200 to 300 square feet, the fuchsia display is one of the smallest, yet one of the most visually captivating displays in the whole garden.

The breadth of fuchsia selections that can be grown in the Northwest astounds visitors, and the fact that the genus *Fuchsia* is a South American plant can be quite a surprise, too. Fuchsia cultivars in the garden represent a cavalcade of hybrids that have been crossed so many times, no one has been able to keep up, but generally parents of the plants available today involve *Fuchsia magellanica*, from Argentina and Chile; *F. fulgens*, from Mexico; and up to perhaps 10 other species. Fuchsia hybridizers have been busy since the late 18th century, when the genus was first brought into cultivation.

In any year there are about 100 fuchsias in the display, many of them hardy throughout a Pacific Northwest winter. Others, such as 'Gartenmeister Bonstedt', get dug up when cold weather threatens. The size of the shrubs runs from diminutive to plants grown as standards, on single trunks, such as the pink and red 'Celia Smedley'.

Eastside Fuchsia Society volunteers maintain the garden, talk with the public, and answer questions. They also will provide fuchsia names for those who haven't picked up the numbered list inside.

Jerry Nissley

As interim curator for the nascent botanical garden and special projects manager for the Bellevue Parks and Recreation Department, Jerry Nissley dealt with the management plans and procedures for the Garden. Because he was involved in the early stages of the Garden, he was able to observe the relationship between the City and the Society. "I remember that we would meet in a small office huddled around a small table," he remembers of the meetings held at the parks department headquarters at Kelsey Creek — "Roy Gatbunton, John Barker and Roger Hoesterey from the City and Nell Scott, Judy Evans, and Iris Jewett from the Society, just to name a few."

Jerry's work was part of the team effort it took to create a world-class garden, he says. Both strong support from the public and commitment from the City to take care of its gardens and parks are part of what makes the Bellevue Botanical Garden unique.

Nissley joined the City in 1988 and works today in the Resource Management Division of Parks and Community Services.

Gardeners can identify whichever selection catches their eyes, such as 'Dying Embers', a single red and purple, or 'Firecracker', which has narrow orange tubular flowers and variegated foliage.

At the garden, it isn't only the sweet flowers that resemble lady's earrings dangling from the stems that attract attention. Many cultivars of fuchsias offer interesting foliage color, too. *F. magellanica* var. *gracilis* 'Variegata' has soft green and cream variegation. The same species also has 'Aurea', which has electric yellow leaves that show off the bicolor flowers of red and purple.

Hardy fuchsias are considered to be *F. magellanica* and hybrids that can survive the generally mild winters in the maritime Pacific Northwest. They are left to overwinter in the ground as any other ornamental shrub, and the only caveat is that, because the plants leaf out rather late in the spring — often not until May — gardeners must be careful that they don't consider their fuchsia to be a dead bundle of twigs and toss it on the compost pile.

ABOVE *Fuchsia* 'Firecracker'
ABOVE RIGHT *Fuchsia* 'Gartenmeister Bonstedt', a
tender selection RIGHT The
Fuchsia Garden is located
near the main entrance
to the visitor center. Visitors are able to match
a fuchsia they see in the
display with a printed list.

ABOVE **Northwest native habitat for both flora and fauna is on display in the Native Discovery Garden.** RIGHT FROM TOP *Ribes sanguineum*, native red-flowering currant; *Blechnum spicant* (deer fern); *Acer circinatum* (vine maple); *Corylus cornuta var. californica* (**Western**

The Native Discovery Garden is south and slightly east of the visitor center along the main loop trail. If visitors take the trail south from the NPA Borders, they will come upon the native garden just before the Yao Japanese Garden. It's a high wooded area, and there is even a secondary path that meanders by a pond.

The Seattle landscape architecture firm of Charles Anderson drew up the plans for the garden, and volunteers planted the area in the winter of 1999. Through the years, members of the East Lake Washington District of Garden Clubs have helped to maintain the garden.

The discovery part of the Native Discovery Garden for many visitors is to learn that there are many natives that make fine garden plants.

The garden illustrates the many layers of plant life in the Northwest, from ground covers to trees. Looking down, *Cornus canadensis* (bunchberry) creeps along; it is a circumboreal species that grows well in the forest duff in the Pacific Northwest. As an ornamental ground cover, it offers small, white, upward-facing spring "flowers" that are really the bracts surrounding its tiny, true flowers just as with one of its larger relatives — and Northwest native — *C. nuttallii.*

Two kinds of shrubby *Vaccinium* grow in the garden. *V. parviflorum* (red huckleberry) sprouts from nurse logs, as it does in the forest, and *V. ovatum* (evergreen huckleberry) holds the lower midcanopy layer, growing well in dry shade here as a native as well as it grows as an ornamental in the Waterwise Garden. *Corylus cornuta* var. *californica* (beaked hazelnut) grows higher, but not as high as the native trees that

provide the canopy for the garden, among them *Acer macrophyllum* (bigleaf maple), *Thuja plicata* (Western red cedar), and *Pseudotsuga menziesii* (Douglas fir).

The interpretive signs in the native garden highlight and explain how and why they grow well in our climate. Gardeners looking for plants that need little supplemental water once they are established can find good choices here — *Acer circinatum* (vine maple), *Blechnum spicant* (deer fern), and *Ribes sanguineum* (red-flowering currant).

As it is with all parts of the garden, the Native Discovery Garden is enjoyed by strollers, plant lovers, and gardeners, as well as photographers and even artists, who set up their easels and paints to capture a quiet scene. And as the stroll continues, the Native Discovery Garden segues into the design and plants along the fence and outside the gates of the Yao Japanese Garden.

LEFT **Northwest nature is on display for visitors who move through the Garden.** BOTTOM **Native ground cover** *Cornus canadensis* **(bunchberry) develops red berries from its flowers, which are tiny and surrounded by white bracts.** FAR LEFT ABOVE **The pond in the native garden is seasonal — growing larger during winter rains and shrinking in the dry summer.** FAR LEFT BELOW **The flowers of the Northwest native** *Trillium ovatum* **age from white to pink.**

LOST MEADOW/LOOP TRAIL

The quiet deepens on the Lost Meadow Loop Trail, which takes off the main loop trail south. Strolling back along the path, which winds a third of a mile through and back to the main loop, visitors see a part of Bellevue that hasn't been seen for many years. It's the result of second growth, after the initial logging occurred at the turn of the 20th century.

The canopy of trees opens out onto a meadow, and the area makes for prime bird-watching or just a place for a quiet lunch, away from the office.

The natural area has grown, and the buffer zone in the Garden has been enlarged, with the March 2006 acquisition of an additional 17 acres next to the Lost Meadow.

RIGHT **Acres of natural area at the Garden allow visitors to experience what Bellevue was like before development.** LEFT TOP **Visitors who spend the day or just a lunch hour in the Garden benefit from some quiet time in the meadow.** LEFT BELOW **The tree canopy provides the upper layer in a Northwest forest, as shown in the forested parts of the Lost Meadow.**

The
Experience

The Experience

"A garden in the woods… in the heart of the city"

The Garden is made; the stage is set. Now what? Public gardens provide not just an amenity in their existence, but also the perfect venue for community activities and fundraising events. At the Bellevue Botanical Garden, the experiences available to visitors are variously entertaining, educational, and enlightening.

DOCENTS

A docent is a valuable link between the public and the Garden, the interpreter of the history and landscape, knowledgeable about everything from plant names — including how to use the plant database — to Cal's penchant for hybridizing rhododendrons.

"Be prepared" should be the motto of the docent program at the Garden. The first class to train those valuable volunteers was held in the summer of 1991, a year before the Garden opened.

Doris Evans and Ann Pryde created the first docent-training program. Eight volunteers took the training. They were a hardy and imaginative group in the first few years of the Garden, because many of their tours consisted of "this is where we will have. ..." Currently, more than 40 volunteers act as docents.

Some visitors to the Garden prefer to be alone, to stroll the paths or study the plants. Many visitors bring out-of-town relatives for an afternoon's activity. But others, especially garden clubs, or small, enthusiastic plant groups, would rather have someone along on their walk through

vance, but docents are on site on weekends to answer questions, and a public tour is conducted each Saturday and Sunday afternoon.

The experience of a knowledgeable docent can make all the difference in a visit to the Garden and can be the reason that visitors return to the Garden, as well as spread the word to friends that the Garden is a great place to visit. Docents, along with the other Garden volunteers, keep the Garden alive.

LIVING LAB

The next generation of gardeners — and Garden visitors — is always in the wings waiting for that spark of interest that leads them to the love of the natural world. The Living Lab program provides that spark to students in kindergarten through fifth grade. Patricia Burgess created the program in 1994, just two years after the Garden opened. Since then, it has entertained, taught, and captured the fancy of children, beginning with 60 the first spring, up to more than 700 in the spring of 2006.

The program was funded mostly through city money and was run by volunteers for the first three years. Then teachers were hired to conduct the lessons, with volunteers close at hand. In 1999, when the City could no longer fund the program, the Society took over and hired Barb Williams to run the Living Lab. After a year off for planning, the program was up and running again.

The Living Lab lessons are graded and meet the specific curricula requirements in science and nature for the Bellevue School District and are aligned with the Washington State Science Essential Learnings. The students' sessions in botany and natural science take a hands-on approach, and they

the Garden — someone who can answer questions, provide historical details, and give insight into the landscape. Docents give visitors more depth to their visit.

To do that, the docents need to know what they are talking about, and that's where training comes in. The eight-week training covers a wide range of topics, from botany to plant identification to the land as it was when the Shorts family lived there. Bits of history help the Garden come alive before the eyes of the visitors.

Training is never really finished, and the docents meet twice a month to learn from one another as well as listen to talks from experts on specific subjects.

Not all docents have the same interest, and so it is of particular note that groups can request someone with deep plant knowledge or extensive historical detail.

Docent tours are scheduled in ad-

delight in seeing how things work in the natural world. Teachers delight in it, too, because the number of classes that sign up for the spring and fall sessions seems to grow each year.

Different children may leave the Living Lab with different memories. Some might be impressed with the work of worms in the soil; others could become fascinated with how flowers are put together. Here's one schoolchild's "take-home message" from the Living Lab:

"I had such fun learning about the Natives and how they used different kinds of plants. I didn't know that Nootka Rose was

made into perfume. Or that baby diapers were made from cedar and that moss was put into it to make it soft. I couldn't imagine my baby sister wearing one of those diapers!"

GARDEN D'LIGHTS

"Lee came to me and said, 'While I don't understand the Garden's huge success, you're doing a great job. Figure out how to get people up here in the winter.'" From Nancy Fonk

It may have seemed like a Judy Garland and Mickey Rooney routine at first — let's put on a little light show. It was a way to draw people into the Garden during the offseason, but has become one of most talked-about "gardens" there. The first Garden d'Lights was made up of white

ABOVE **Workshops are held through the year to build or repair displays for Garden d'Lights.** BELOW **The light display that represents the NPA Bor-**ders leads many visitors to an impromptu plant identification session. RIGHT **All ages marvel in the light display during the holiday season.**

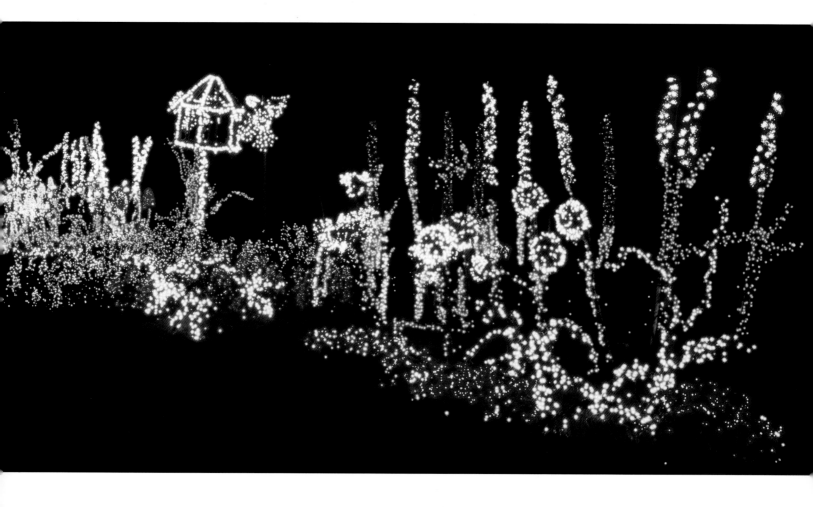

ABOVE **Garden d'Lights begins each day just as the sun goes down.**
LEFT **Volunteers spend thousands of hours creating and setting up the light displays.**
RIGHT **The annual Mother's Day tea kicks off the Garden's year.**

mini-lights decorating shrubs and trees, but the spotlight was on the amazing wisteria arbor, with its clusters of purple "flowers" dangling from green stems. The winter newsletter from the Society noted that "the display will be expanded yearly." That could be called an understatement.

The first Garden d'Lights in 1994 drew between 1,000 and 1,500 people. By 1996, that number was between 7,000 and 9,000, and the following year it jumped to 32,000. At last count in 2005, 80,000 visitors enjoyed the holiday show. Going to see the lights became an event for the evening, as music and refreshments were added to the schedule.

So popular was the first event that Denise Lane remembers that more than 500 people requested information on how to make flowers from lights. This interest led to the first light-making classes, which have been held every year since.

Volunteers brainstormed new ideas for displays. In 1997, about a dozen volunteers took a class from Elizabeth Price-Asher, who had created the wisteria arbor in lights; she taught them the technique of bundling the lights. Currently, classes and workshops are held almost year-round to get ready for the event, led by Udell Fresk. In 2005, 310 volunteers put in more than 4,000 hours to make Garden d'Lights the show-stopping event that it is. It has become an art to learn how to carefully bundle and wrap the cords of lights in particular patterns that produce a flower or plant that is actually identifiable.

From the wisteria arbor, more lights grew. A pink rhododendron appeared, and a rose trellis on the side of the Sharp cabin was part of the display within two years. One of the most noticeable additions to the lights was the NPA Border. Could a

garden of lights be made that reflected the beauty of the border? It could, and after hundreds of volunteer hours, visitors to Garden d'Lights could be seen standing on the patio in the dark, astounded to see the border glowing across the lawn. Conversation among visitors included enthusiastic plant-identification sessions: "Look, delphiniums!" "Is that phlox?"

Today, visitors don't just stand on the patio and look; they also walk down a trail to view garden lights. Children enjoy the spider, slug, and frog while adults are impressed with the laburnum walk, its long streams of yellow "flowers" modeled after Rosemary Verey's at Barnsley House in England. A lily pond, poinsettia tree, pampas grass are all part of the delightful light show that has become the biggest event in the entire year of the Garden.

MOTHER'S DAY

Spring in the Garden can be a chancy thing in the Pacific Northwest, but spring

is what draws us out into the Garden, and the pairing of a garden event with a celebration of Mother's Day seems natural.

The first Mother's Day tea took place in 1993 and drew 1,000 people. Each year, visitors come to stroll the paths and enjoy the blooms of rhododendrons and magnolias, along with the emerging foliage of the Garden. Beautiful flowering shrubs play backdrop to the photos of Mom or Grandma with children or extended families. It's considered the unofficial opening of the garden year — in a garden that never closes.

POPS IN THE PARK

Pops in the Park was held in August 1992, the summer the Garden opened. People were drawn to the music and the chance to enjoy the outdoors while check-

ing out the new landscapes of the Bellevue Botanical Garden.

Since then, Pops in the Park has been held annually the first Saturday in August. Accompanied by music, and free to those attending, the event gives visitors an entirely new appreciation for the Garden.

AUCTION

Fundraising can be fun, as is evident each year at the auction. The first one, held in 1991, may have been a modest affair compared with today's standards, but the spirit of the event has remained a constant.

It began with a silent auction only, but the live component, added later and continued to today, brings a festive air to the gathering. And the auction items have

always held great interest, whether it's an oil change or a cruise — or one of June Willard's apple pies, which have appeared almost every year. In the early years, June recalls, she made the pies with apples from Cal's orchard, and Cal — Cal and Harriet always bought two tables at the auction — made sure he went home with one of the pies. When he was outbid one year, he followed the next by slapping on a high bid at the start.

Recently, a theme was taken up that started several years ago, when a rare plant auction was added to the event. "Rare" became a recurring idea. The auction was denoted as a "Rare Affair," which reflects not only the items offered, but also the enthusiasm and enjoyment of all involved.

ABOVE **Every auction has its own theme; here it was "Rare Affair — Casablanca."** BELOW **The evening includes entertainment, in addition to silent and** live bidding. LEFT **Pops in the Park shows off both the Garden and the Pacific Northwest climate to perfection.**

Seasonal Highlights

No matter the season, the Bellevue Botanical Garden offers visitors an interesting landscape. The scenes change as the months go by, and the highlights move from one plant combination or garden view to another, but the true test of a garden is passed: There is always something to enjoy.

Here is a sampling of what is in bloom or of interest in the gardens during each season.

SPRING

NORTHWEST PERENNIAL ALLIANCE BORDERS
Aesculus pavia
Camassia leichtlinii 'Blue Danube'
Epimedium x cantabrigiense
Fritillaria meleagris
Geum triflorum 'Prairie Smoke'
Helleborus argutifolius
Helleborus foetidus
Lamium orvala 'Album'
Lathyrus vernus
Narcissus bulbocodium
Narcissus 'Pipit'
Pulmonaria saccarata 'Mrs. Moon'

YAO JAPANESE GARDEN
Asarum caudatum
Cornus controversa 'Pagoda'
Darmera peltata
Mahonia repens
Primula kisoana
Rhododendron kiusianum
Trochodendron aralioides
Viburnum plicatum 'Roseum'

SHORTS GROUND COVER GARDEN
Dicentra formosa 'Adrian Bloom'
Fothergilla gardenii

SUMMER

NORTHWEST PERENNIAL ALLIANCE BORDERS
Agastache 'Apricot Sprite'
Billardiera longifolia
Campanula cochlearifolia 'Elizabeth Oliver'
Campanula lactiflora
Cerinthe major 'Purpurescens'
Cersium rivulare 'Atropurpureum'
Chaerophyllum hirsutum 'Roseum'
Crocosmia 'Lucifer'
Eryngium amethystinum
Geranium psilostemon
Geum 'Georgenburg'
Rosa glauca 'Carmenetta'

YAO JAPANESE GARDEN
Arisaema heterophyllum
Cornus kousa var. chinensis 'Milky Way'
Elaeocarpus decipiens
Hakonechloa macra 'Aureola'
Hydrangea paniculata 'Grandiflora'
Nandina domestica 'Filementosa'
Polygonatum x hybridum
Spiraea japonica 'Little Princess'

SHORTS GROUND COVER GARDEN
Astilbe 'Sprite'
Campanula poscharskyana 'Blue Waterfall'

FALL

NORTHWEST PERENNIAL ALLIANCE BORDERS
Aconitum carmichaelii 'Kelmscott'
Aster lateriflorus 'Lady in Black'
Eupatorium rugosum 'Chocolate'
Helianthus salicifolius
Hydrangea macrophylla 'Amethyst'
Impatiens omeiana
Nicotiana mutabilis
Sorbus reducta
Uncinia uncinata

YAO JAPANESE GARDEN
Acer japonicum 'Aconitifolium'
Acer palmatum
Ardisia japonica
Heptacodium miconioides
Miscanthus sinensis 'Yaku Jima'
Stewartia pseudocamellia

SHORTS GROUND COVER GARDEN
Acer buergerianum
Acer griseum
Acer triflorum
Euonymus europaeus 'Aldenhamensis'
Mahonia x media 'Lionel Fortescue'

WINTER

NORTHWEST PERENNIAL ALLIANCE BORDERS
Arum italicum ssp. italicum 'Marmoratum' (syn. Arum italicum 'Pictum')
Carex testacea
Helleborus x hybridus
Helleborus orientalis

YAO JAPANESE GARDEN
Acer davidii
Callicapra dichotoma 'Issai'
Chimonanthus praecox var. luteus
Corylopsis pauciflora
Mahonia aquifolium
Polygonatum x hybridum

Gaultheria mucronata 'Rubra'
(syn. Pernettya mucronata 'Rubra')
Leucothoe fontanesiana 'Rollissonii'
Lindera erythrocarpa
Lorapetalum chinense f. rubrum 'Razzleberri'
Prunus x yedoensis 'Akebono'
Trillium kurabayashii
Zenobia pulverulenta 'Raspberry Ripple'

WATERWISE GARDEN
Akebia quinata
Anemone nemorosa

Berberis buxifolia 'Nana'
Berberis thunbergii 'Atropurpurea Nana'
Cistus x hybridus
Cotinus coggygria 'Royal Purple'
Corylus colurna
Doronicum pardalianches
Iris sibirica
Lamium galeobdolon 'Hermann's Pride'
Nepeta 'Dropmore'
Osmanthus delavayi
Rosa rugosa 'Alba'
Tanacetum parthenium 'Aureum'

ENTRANCE GARDEN
Abutilon vitifolium
Calycanthus floridus
Cercis chinensis
Fothergilla gardenii 'Blue Mist'
Leucothoe walteri 'Nana'
Osmanthus decorus
Phlomis fruticosa
Stephanandra incisa 'Crispa'

ALPINE ROCK GARDEN
Allium crenulatum
Aquilegia flavescens
Armeria maritima 'Rubrifolia'
Aubrieta olympica
Berberis thunbergii 'Bagatelle'

Campanula portenschlagiana
Erodium chrysanthum
Erythronium 'Pagoda'
Euphorbia myrsinites
Gentiana acaulis
Iris cristata
Penstemon pinifolius 'Iron Man'
Pulsatilla vulgaris
Primula 'Jay-Jay'

NATIVE DISCOVERY GARDEN
Amelanchier alnifolia 'Smokey'
Lysichiton americanum
Ribes x gordonianum

Ceratostigma griffithii
Crambe cordifolia
Euphorbia griffithii 'Fireglow'
Geranium x cantabrigiense 'Biokovo'
Geranium pratense Victor Reiter strain
Geranium 'Philippe Vapelle'
Gillenia trifolia
Hydrangea serrata 'Shirotae'
Lobelia cardinalis
Molinia caerulea ssp. caerulea 'Variegata'

WATERWISE GARDEN
Cornus alba 'Elegantissima'
Dierama pulcherrimum

Echinacea purpurea 'Bravado'
Erigeron karvinskianus
Hydrangea quercifolia
Knifophia citrina
Lonicera pileata
Phygelius 'Moonraker'
Stipa arundinacea (syn. Anemanthele lessoniana)

ENTRANCE GARDEN
Aster x frikartii 'Monch'
Ceanothus x pallidus 'Marie Simon'
Clematis heracleifolia
Clethra alnifolia 'Hummingbird'
Itea virginica 'Henry's Garnet'
Phormium 'Jack Spratt'

Potentilla nepalensis 'Miss Willmott'

ALPINE ROCK GARDEN
Allium ceruum
Antirrhinum sempervirens
Callirhoe involucrata
Campanula carpatica
Ceratostigma plumbaginoides
Daboecia cantabrica 'Rainbow'
Delosperma basuticum
Digitalis obscura
Erigeron speciosus
Geranium dalmaticum
Geranium sanguineum
Geum triflorum var. campanulatum

NATIVE DISCOVERY GARDEN
Cornus canadensis
Cornus stolonifera 'Flaviramea'

LOST MEADOW TRAIL
Clethra barbinervis
Cornus canadensis
Itea japonica 'Beppu'

Molinia careulea
Oxydendrum arboreum
Symphoricarpos x doorenbosii 'Magic Berry'
Vaccinium corymbosum 'Sunshine Blue'

WATERWISE GARDEN
Aster divaricatus
Cercidiphyllum japonicum
Koelreuteria paniculata
Miscanthus sinensis 'Strictus'
Salix purpurea 'Nana'
Viburnum tinus 'Spring Bouquet'
Viburnum trilobum 'Wentworth'

ALPINE GARDEN
Acer circinatum
Berberis thunbergii 'Atropurpurea Nana'
Calluna vulgaris 'Sesam'
Ceratostigma plumbaginoides
Imperata cylindrica 'Rubra'
Sedum spurium 'Schorbuser Blut'
Taxodium disticum 'Peve Minaret'
Zauschneria californica

ENTRANCE GARDEN
Anemone hupehensis
Aronia melanocarpa
Carex elata 'Bowles Golden'
Caryopteris incana
Fothergilla gardenii 'Blue Mist'

Osmanthus heterophyllus 'Gulftide'
Parrotia persica
Spiraea 'Anthony Waterer'
Stokesia laevis 'Blue Danube'

LOST MEADOW TRAIL
Aronia melanocarpa 'Autumn Magic'

FUCHSIA GARDEN
'Army Nurse'
'Aurea'
Fuchsia encliandra
'Little Beauty'
F. magellanica var. gracilis
'Mephisto'

'Painted Desert'
'Peaches and Cream'
'President'
'Viola'

SHORTS GROUND COVER GARDEN
Acer griseum
Bergenia cordifolia 'Winterglut' ('Winter Glow')
Betula albosinensis var. septentrionalis
Callicarpa bodinieri var. giraldii 'Profusion'
Garrya elliptica 'Evie'

Hamamelis x intermedia 'Arnold Promise'
Photinia davidiana var. undulata

WATERWISE GARDEN
Cornus mas
Corylus colurna
Elaeagnus x ebbingei 'Gilt Edge'
Epimedium pinnatum ssp. colchicum

Lonicera pileata
Myrica californica

ALPINE GARDEN
Juniperus horizontalis 'Grey Forest'
Vaccinium vitis-idaea var. minus

ENTRANCE GARDEN
Corylopsis spicata

Hamamelis mollis
Lonicera standishii
Osmanthus heterophyllus 'Goshiki'
Taxus cuspidata 'Monloo'

Timeline

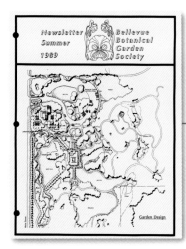

1981	Cal and Harriet Shorts donate land to the City of Bellevue
1984	The first meeting of people interested in creating a botanical garden
	Bellevue Botanical Garden Society formed
1989	Original design and master plan completed, the Sharp cabin moved
	Groundbreaking
1991	The first docent class meets
1992	June 27, the Garden opens, Shorts Visitor Center, Northwest Perennial Alliance Border, Shorts Ground Cover Garden, Fuchsia Garden
1993	January, Inauguration Day windstorm
1994	Dedication of Yao Japanese Garden
	Living Lab program begins
	Dedication of Waterwise Garden
	First Garden d'Lights
1996	Master plan review
1997	Harriet Shorts dies
	Dedication of Alpine Rock Garden
1999	Native Plant Garden
2002	June, 10th anniversary, Ground Cover Garden rededication
2003	Cal Shorts dies
2006	March, 17 acres added to the garden
2007	June, 15th-anniversary celebration

Index

ACKNOWLEDGMENTS

We thank the BBG book committee — Norm Hansen, Nancy Fonk, Nancy Daar, June Willard, Linda Urbaniak, Anna Littlewood, Jan Simonton, Debbie Vaught, and Nancy Harvey — for choosing Garden Bench Books to produce *The Bellevue Botanical Garden: Celebrating the First 15 Years* and for their support throughout the process. We spent an enjoyable year living through 22 years of the Garden's past.

In addition, Marty thanks those BBGS members and others who made a trip down memory lane to help re-create the history of the Garden: Iris and Bob Jewett, Iain Robertson, Lee Springgate, Pat Roome, Charles Price and Glenn Withey, Bob Lilly, Carrie Becker, Tom Kuykendall, and Patricia Burgess.

Anyone who has visited the Garden carries away mental images of favorite scenes, but unearthing good photographs of what happened is another thing altogether. This book could not have been done without the contribution of these outstanding professional photographers: Lynne Harrison, Allan Mandell, Sandra Lee Reha, Andrew Drake, and Rob Cardillo. Virginia gratefully acknowledges those volunteers whose photos have made a difference, including Joanne White and the members of Genus II. A special thanks goes to Judy Panjeti. Many people at the City of Bellevue helped with photos, especially Jan Simonton at the Garden. Thanks to June Willard for taking photos from the beginning, and saving them.

Marty Wingate and Virginia Hand

PHOTOGRAPHY CREDITS

Multiple page items are identified from upper left corner, rotating clockwise, a–f.

Rob Cardillo: 47c, 72b–c

City of Bellevue: 26, 29b–c, 33c, 34b, 47d, 61, 69e, 73b, 74a, 79a, 84a, 87d, 89a, 90b, 101, 102, 103a–b

City of Bellevue Public Art Program: 33b, e, & f

City of Bellevue Utilities: 66a, 68, 69b–d, 70a–b, 71a–c, 97c

Collection of Bellevue Botanical Garden: 17, 18b, 27

Nancy Daar: 95, 96

Andrew Drake: 40, 69a,

Eastside Heritage Center: 16a–c

Virginia Hand: 59b

Lynne Harrison: 6, 19, 20, inset 31, 32a & inset, 35, 41, 47b, 52, 53a–b, 60b, 64, 65a & c, 72a, 73a, 75b–c, 80a, 81a & c, 82, 85a–c, 87a–c, 88a, 89b, 90a, 91, 98b, 99, 100a

Terry Hayes: 28

Anna Littlewood: 34a

Allan Mandell: 8, 38–39, 45b, 46, 49a–b, 51, 76b, 77

Sandra Lee Reha: cover front and back, inside covers, 2–3, 22, 24, 29a, 44, 47a, 48a–b, 50, 55, 56b, 57, 58a, 59a, 66b, 67, 83, 84b, 86, 107

Jo Anne Rosen: 14, 27b

The Genus II Group at BBG: Elliott Brogren 42b; Peter Martin 42a, c, &d; Judy Panjeti cover flaps, front and back, 5, 33a & d, 56a, 64, 63b, 74b, 75a, 79b, 81b, 98a, 100b; Rebecca Randall 58b, 60a, 78, 94; Rocky Rockwell 43, 62, 65b, 80b, 88b; Joanne White 31; Bill Willard 92–93

Bill and June Willard: 11a-f, 12-13, 15, 18a, 27a, 45a, 54a-c, 63a, 76a

Barb Williams: 97a–b.

ILLUSTRATION CREDITS

Jongejan Gerrard McNeal (JGM): 25
Iain Robertson: 30
Jean Hoxter: map 37

QUOTE ATTRIBUTIONS

Page 14: Lee Springgate, quoting Harriet Shorts obituary, *The Seattle Times,* January 2, 1997
Page 36: posted above Nancy Fonk's desk
Page 72: Lee Springgate, phone interview
Page 94: from a BBG brochure

Produced by Garden Bench Books, Llc, for
The Bellevue Botanical Garden Society

ISBN 978-0-9793221-0-5
ISBN 0-9793221-0-3

Library of Congress Control Number: 2007921778

Written by Marty Wingate
Designed by Virginia Hand
Copy-edited by Leighton Wingate
Index by Andrea Avni at Vashon Island WordWrights
Prepress services by iocolor, Seattle
Printed by C & C Offset Printing Co. Ltd., China

Published and distributed by
Bellevue Botanical Garden Society
12001 Main Street
Bellevue, WA 98005
(425) 452-2750

www.bellevuebotanical.org